Peace by Peace

MOVEMENT RHETORIC/RHETORIC'S MOVEMENTS

Victoria J. Gallagher

MOVEMENT
RHETORIC
RHETORIC'S MOVEMENTS

Also of Interest

Activist Literacies: Transnational Feminisms and Social Media Rhetorics,
   Jennifer Nish

*The Democratic Ethos: Authenticity and Instrumentalism in US Movement
   Rhetoric after Occupy*, A. Freya Thimsen

Liturgy of Change: Rhetorics of the Civil Rights Meeting, Elizabeth Ellis
   Miller

PEACE
BY
PEACE

Risking Public Action,
Creating Social Change

LISA ELLEN SILVESTRI

THE UNIVERSITY OF
SOUTH CAROLINA PRESS

Published by the University of South Carolina Press
Columbia, South Carolina 29208

uscpress.com

Printed in the United States of America

Library of Congress Cataloging-in-Publication Data can be found at
https://lccn.loc.gov/2024031917.

ISBN: 978-1-64336-519-0 (hardcover)
ISBN: 978-1-64336-520-6 (paperback)
ISBN: 978-1-64336-521-3 (ebook)

To Jane and Arlo

Be joyful though you have considered all the facts.

—WENDELL BERRY, MANIFESTO

CONTENTS

LIST OF ILLUSTRATIONS

SERIES EDITOR'S PREFACE

The University of South Carolina series "Movement Rhetoric/Rhetoric's Movements" builds on the Press's long-standing reputation in the field of rhetoric and communication and its cross-disciplinary commitment to studies of civil rights and civil justice. Books in the series address two central questions: In historical and contemporary eras characterized by political, social, and economic movements enacted through rhetorical means, how—and with what consequences—are individuals, collectives, and institutions changed and transformed? How, and to what extent, can analyses of rhetoric's movements in relation to circulation and uptake help point the way to a more equal and equitable world?

In this engaging and timely monograph, Lisa Ellen Silvestri examines our human capacity for peace by showcasing smaller scale, achievable peace acts carried out by everyday people. She contextualizes this work in relation to the contemporary condition of drift, characterized by dislocation, fragmentation, and disconnection, and *phronesis*, characterized as the capacity to discern a practical course of action, one that preserves noble or ethical values, in unusual or complicated situations. Each of the cases in the book illuminates phronesis as the capacity to acknowledge the uncertainties and struggles of life and yet be compelled toward positive action anyway. The book is meant to not offer solutions but rather offer templates that introduce alternative modes of engagement in contemporary civic life; that is, modes that can be utilized by all of us. This accessible and hugely compelling book is for academic and nonacademic readers alike and a significant addition to the series.

PREFACE

Well, I've got a hammer
And I've got a bell
And I've got a song to sing
All over this land

—PETE SEEGER AND LEE HAYS, *IF I HAD A HAMMER*, 1962

Without knowing it, I've been writing this book for a long time. Since childhood, really. Thanks to my parents, I grew up listening to the folk music of Woody and Arlo Guthrie, Lead Belly, Pete Seeger, Bob Dylan, Joan Baez, and Peter, Paul and Mary. Their songs taught me about the hopes, sorrows, values, and beliefs of ordinary people living everyday lives. The folk tradition recounts our human history as ramblers and tells of our inborn interconnectedness with each other and with the earth. Recurrent themes usually involve love, war, longing, justice, death, and family. Stories like the ones relayed through folk music are ostensibly authorless; handed down from generation to generation serving as signposts to navigate life. As a kid, singing along felt like an exercise in recitation, a way of not forgetting so I wouldn't get lost.

For forty years I've been singing the same songs, revisiting the same ideas, dog-earing the same pages, writing the same notes to myself, and coming back to the same realizations. This book is an outcome of that process. It's not the end of it, of course, just another one of my attempts to build a cairn of temporary understanding about what it is we are supposed to be doing here. Now, I don't claim to be a troubadour, but I wrote this book in honor of the folk tradition.[1] In it, I tell you about some people I've met who are carrying out the human project in ways that align with a folkloric invocation of the human spirit. They are regular people engaged in localized, right action on behalf of a greater good. The book captures the conversations I had with those people, but the process of writing it has felt more like a conversation with myself. More specifically, an imaginary conversation with my kids. It is part personal reflection, part critical theory, part ethnographic account, and part prayer. A medley, by heart.

As you read, you will notice that I use the word *person* as opposed to "*individual.*" That is a deliberate choice. The individual is an isolated unit—what academics call "a neoliberal subject"—functioning and acting alone. The person, however, can never be properly understood outside the framework of social relationships and obligations. Theologian and peace activist Thomas Merton writes that a person's reason for existence is not survival, efficiency, or competition, but "truth, justice, love, and liberty." In his words, fulfillment comes through "being called to collaborate with others in building a world of security and peace."[2] Leave it to a monk to point out how much we need each other. In this respect, I occasionally refer to *we* and *us* to denote the generalized human person. I know generalizations are fraught, their implications presumptuous, unfair, and even hurtful. Please forgive me. I appreciate your generous reading.

I also owe a heap of gratitude to the scholars, activists, artists, and changemakers who I reference in these pages. I hope my representation of you and your work reflects my esteem. If I could, I would formally reference all the people who sourced my motivation for this book but many of those ideas came out of conversations over beers, in car rides, on hiking trails, in phone calls or by electronic mail. Nonetheless here's my attempt—Mike Briggs, David Depew, Beka and Charlie Wilkins-Pepiton, Ron Large, Robbie Newell, Carol Myers, Kathryn Wehr, Mat Rude, Aubrey Purdy, and Renu Pariyadath. I hope you can hear some of yourself in this book. To the LDP: Caitlin Bruce, Heather Woods, Emily Winderman, Michaela Frischherz, and Kim Singletary, and to my friend Casey Schmitt for your honest feedback and for pushing me to bring my voice forward in my writing. I haven't published anything in the last five years without your support, so thank you for being my first audience and my security blanket. To Emma VanderWeyst for your help transcribing the interviews. Thanks to Aurora Bell and Victoria Gallagher for listening to my idea and taking a chance on this uncommon project, to the anonymous reviewers, and the whole production team. And finally, this book wouldn't exist without the people I interviewed for it, especially the ones who became chapters—Shawn, Curtis, Gidon, Estelle, Nawal, Ralph, Shannon, Drew, and Keith. I think you are amazing. You are doing the type of work we should all be doing. Thank you.

I am also deeply humbled and enormously indebted to the people who have had to live with me during this book's creation. Jane, my stated muse.

Thank you for making me laugh every day and reminding me about poetry. Arlo, you came in clutch, right when I needed you. Thank you for your tenderness and good listening. And Peter, my compass, and my co-conspirator. Thank you for helping me travel, tolerating my moods, taking me on walks, and indulging my midnight soliloquies. What would I do without you?

Introduction

Crowdsourcing Hope

Out on the edge of darkness there rides a peace train.

—CAT STEVENS, *PEACE TRAIN*, 1971

In the summer of 2018, I became a mother. Those who are familiar with the gamut of parenthood might remember well the early days of fatigue, isolation, and throat-choking vulnerability. From the window of our "milking bunker" (my droll reference to the nursery), my newborn and I looked out onto a particularly bleak world. Forest fires engulfed the western United States where we lived at the time. Everything outside our window appeared in an eerie sepia tone like an old-timey photograph. There were no birds, no squirrels, just trees holding their ground and struggling to breathe. The smoky haze made it difficult to see our mailbox at the end of the driveway. The city issued an order for residents to "Stay home, Stay safe."[1] These were the years leading up to the global pandemic when everyone would come to experience the bitter taste of confinement.

I listened to news on the radio as I traipsed from room to room in an exhausted beast-like stupor. I will tell you this—the news was not good. The Trump administration's zero-tolerance policy on immigration meant US authorities were separating thousands of children from their parents at the southern border, Robert Mueller was investigating possible collusion between Trump and Russia during the 2016 Presidential election, Dr. Christine Blasey Ford was alleging that Supreme Court nominee Brett Kavanaugh sexually assaulted her when they were teenagers, Facebook got caught in a data mining scandal involving Cambridge Analytica, there were mass shootings in high schools in Florida and Texas, a bar in southern California, and a synagogue in Pittsburgh (just to name a few), and, of course, the devastating wildfires out West raised grave concerns about the state of the climate. And this was just the national news.[2]

I looked at my daughter's wide, expectant eyes then out at the trees. "What have I done?" As quickly as it surfaced, I rejected the thought. It was brief, but it served its purpose. It was asking me to confront what I felt too tired to admit—*This will simply not do.* I thought of those mothers who lift cars off their children. Did you know it's called hysterical strength?[3]

Listening to the news was draining so I switched it off and jumped online. I needed to see and hear some good things. I wanted levity and hope. I had heard of people who watch cat videos for this reason.[4] But I already had a cat. And, as if he knew what I was thinking, he lifted his head and squinted at me from across the room. No, cats weren't going to save us.

I decided to reach out. I opened my email account and clicked new message. At first, the blinking cursor taunted me because I had no plan. All that came to mind was the line from Rufus and Chaka Khan's 1974 hit single, *Tell Me Something Good.* Okay, so I had a subject line. Then I started populating the recipient list. I found myself smiling as I cobbled together some of the most artful, poetic, and engaged people I knew. To me, they were a merry band of hell raisers. They were people who asked big questions and listened hard for small answers. I wondered—Did they know of anyone doing cool things? Positive things? If so, could they tell me about them? I wanted to hear about radical, world-making projects. I needed to hear about them. I clicked send and waited.

And that's basically how it started—my plan to crowdsource hope. I admit I didn't have a specific vision of what I was looking for, but I had a general idea. For fifteen years I had written almost exclusively about war. It's a destructive enterprise, the absolute lowest expression of our humanity. At the heart of my fascination with war is its onset. What drives humans to war? More than that, knowing what we know about the horrors of war, why do we keep doing it? I'm not sure I will ever arrive at a satisfying answer to the latter question but spending so much time thinking about the former helped me turn a corner in my scholarship. Motivations for war became quite boring and ultimately predictable after a while. Fear, power, and competition pretty much sum it up. Not to mention, war itself has become ordinary. America, after all, had been at war in Afghanistan for two decades. War was starting to look like any other large-scale government project—expensive and long term with no firm end date.[5] The routinization of war made peace, as a subject for study, all the more compelling to me. As a conceptual counterpart to war, peace is not the mere absence of war;

it is a positive condition, one that is actively built from the ground up. To make peace—to construct conditions that support human and planetary flourishing—requires engaging with the world in a way that is imaginative, collaborative, and sometimes even quirky, or mischievous.

To my delight, once I stopped giving my attention to war and our capacity for belligerence, I started to see evidence of our capacity for peace. The contexts I studied were still bleak—endless war, joblessness, and, eventually, the pandemic—but I kept finding bright spots; the playful ways humans were muddling through. I even tried my hand at cultivating some of these conditions when, together with community veterans, we enriched the cut-and-dried war story by introducing alternative storytelling formats. Veterans voiced their war experiences through poetry, comic strips, mixed media projects, and six-word short stories.[6] It was powerful and honest. In hindsight what the project did was reveal the dynamism of veteran voice and presence in our community beyond park statues, parades, and bumper stickers. It was some of the most challenging and, therefore, meaningful work I had ever done. I wanted to do more work like that and the next time I hoped to experience less nagging imposter syndrome and creative burnout. I wondered how others doing this type of work maintained their endurance and dealt with feelings of insecurity. These were some of the answers I was looking for when I opened my laptop on that sad summer day. I thought that if I could find projects like these and meet with their creators to learn from them, I could delineate a set of imitable characteristics.

I didn't have a specific outcome in mind. My imagination conjured some sort of guidebook for do-gooders. Publication seemed like a given because I knew the stories would be worth sharing, yet I was open to possibilities for what that could mean. Maybe a podcast? Or a graphic novel? A playbook or travel log? An academic monograph just didn't make sense. The stories needed to exist in the open air, circulating and percolating among people who need to hear them; everyday people trying their best to do right in the world.[7]

So, I hope you find this strange little book instructive, invigorating, and inspiring. It uncovers, through interview-based storytelling, some recurrent attributes of people who went ahead and did a good thing when they didn't have to. One person you will meet, for example, is Estelle Brown, a woman in her seventies who became so fed up with her town's food scarcity that she began planting fruits and vegetables in unused lots, in median strips along the road, and even in the town's cemetery. Each chapter, eight in all, showcases a story like Estelle's—a story about an ordinary person who built something new and lifegiving in the world. What the people in this book do is deceptively radical. That is, their approach is not especially difficult; but it somehow fundamentally transforms an existing paradigm. Instead of telling the stories of political icons like Martin Luther King Jr. or Mother Theresa whose mythic status through "Santa Clausification" has rendered them inimitable, this book showcases smaller-scale, achievable peace acts carried out by everyday people.[8] Because they are everyday people, their efforts are not perfect. The idea here is not to offer solutions but to offer templates that introduce alternative modes of engagement. Then we use those examples as opportunities to think through questions of access, mobility, voice, identity, knowledge, and authority. This book, like the people and projects it discusses, emphasizes process over outcome.

My hope is that these stories act as a lighthouse amid a dark sea of negativity, pointing past the inaction fostered by cynicism toward a rational real-world optimism that change, good change, is not impossible. In the words of feminist poet Adrienne Rich, "We cannot wait to speak until we are perfectly clear and righteous."[9] And we cannot know everything before we take action. Each of us struggles every day to define and defend our sense of purpose and integrity, to justify our existence on the planet, and to understand, if only within our own hearts, who we are and what we believe in. The people featured in this book talk about how they were able to squint through the smog of adult life and do something real. What we take away are vital lessons about the value of humility and delegation, the role of positional knowing and tacit forms of knowledge, the merits of practicality in the wake of structural instability, and the importance of investing in possibility.

Crowdsourcing as Method

In the last decade, scholars from across the disciplines have begun exploring the merits and limitations of crowdsourcing as a research method.[10] The term itself emerged in 2006 from *Wired* magazine writer Jeff Howe who used the term crowdsourcing to describe the increasingly popular business practice of "outsourcing to a large crowd of people."[11] Today crowdsourcing can take many forms including crowdfunding (e.g., donating money to fund a project), crowd labor (e.g., digitizing out-of-print books), and crowd research (e.g., responding to surveys). Due to its wide application in a variety of fields, crowdsourcing today refers to "a digital process employed to obtain information, ideas, and solicit contributions of work, creativity, etc., from large online crowds."[12] Generally speaking, the crowd (which is a contentious topic in scholarly circles because of its ambiguity) refers to a large group of people accessed through the internet.[13] There may be *unbounded* crowds and *bounded* crowds—the former consisting of anonymous individuals, the latter describing a known group. When I wrote an email to a curated list of recipients, I solicited a bounded crowd.

My attraction to crowdsourcing stemmed from the nature of my inquiry. I felt overwhelmed by the litany of what I perceived to be human-created (and -sustained) problems. More than that, I was disheartened by what I experienced as apathy among family, friends, and students. Didn't anyone care? Shouldn't human-created problems be met with human-generated solutions? Surely someone somewhere was doing something. So, I turned to the crowd; specifically, a bounded crowd of scholars, activists, and artists who could tell me if they knew anyone or if anyone in their networks knew anyone positively responding to the world's problems. From a methodological perspective, crowdsourcing is an efficient way to tap a dispersed, collective intelligence.[14]

My subject pool emerged from a preexisting organic social network, and I cannot overlook the role of social capital in this process because the nature of my existing relationship with individual crowd-taskers directly informed the quality and quantity of the referrals I received. If members of the bounded crowd felt goodwill toward me, if they felt compelled by my research interests, if they understood the needs I expressed in the prompt, and if they did, in fact, have a robust social network to tap on my behalf, then I was more likely to draw referrals. In all, I received about a dozen usable referrals. After verifying their eligibility in terms of fit, I engaged them by phone, email, or messaging app. Then I scheduled interviews. Each interview except for two occurred in person and lasted approximately one hour.[15] I controlled the sample to include an array of participants to ensure they reflected what I thought to embody the general characteristics of the phenomenon I was studying. The boundaries of the phenomenon became clearer with each interview and clearer still during the transcription process. I started to notice how each person demonstrated a critical self-awareness, attending to extant power dynamics and disparities in resources and representation. During analysis, I could recognize discrete patterns and themes across all the interviews and a theory emerged.

The research process I just described is what academics call *grounded theory* because a researcher is basically building theory from the ground up (rather than testing or applying theory). Grounded theory is an approach to inquiry that involves inductive reasoning and comparative analysis. The process is iterative and interactive because the researcher must remain open to all possible theoretical understandings and develop only tentative interpretations about what she is seeing before she goes on to collect more data to verify and refine. Once she feels confident that the data is not telling her anything new or different, she can say she reached *saturation*.[16]

I reached saturation in January 2020. The theory I was working on had to do with the value of showing up. But then, in March, the World Health Organization announced the emergence of the global COVID-19 pandemic and told everyone to stay home. Like others who were lucky enough to keep their jobs and work from home, my daily routine consisted of trying to keep a toddler occupied while I carried on with my professional duties. So, for two years, during the peak(s) of the pandemic, my research notes, transcriptions, and tentative theory hung idly in the cloud waiting for a day when I had more time and mental bandwidth to process them. All the while I continued to think, write, and publish peer-reviewed research on ideas related to public performances of showing up. One article I published in *The International Journal of Cultural Studies* explored the contemporary renaissance of nihilism as an indicator of civic mindfulness.[17] What I learned from writing that piece was that people did care, they just couldn't see how to affect positive change. Another essay I wrote for *Rhetoric and Public Affairs* explored coalition-building among historically disparate groups.[18] I looked at how military veterans and Indigenous activists redressed historical trauma enough to build a working trust so they could align against the construction of an oil pipeline through the Standing Rock Reservation. Theory-wise, these pieces were like sharks circling the same waters. I wanted to know what it means to show up in the context of late modernity. I was finding that showing up meant accepting your interconnectivity with others, understanding your fit in terms of agency, and readying yourself for action in the face of uncertainty. The opposite of showing up—feeling lost, alone, and powerless—is the experience of what some scholars refer to as *drift*.[19]

Conditions of Drift

Drift, or feelings of "aimless inner floating," is a symptom of our late-modern, post-industrial age.[20] As sociologists tell it, the basic story is that through processes of industrialization, globalization, and automation, the economy shifted from the production of tangible goods such as cars and furniture to the production of intangible goods such as influence and advice-giving.[21] Consequently, the value and importance of blue-collar unionized work fell away and more people began going to college, which ultimately allowed them to experience higher salaries, stronger social mobility, and reduced working hours. On its face, more autonomy and self-determination doesn't sound too bad, but as people moved up and out, they also moved away from the sense of identity and belonging that came with membership in traditional social groups such as religious congregations, unions, political parties, or professional groups.

An effect of all this relocation is a troubling sense of dislocation. Sociologist Zygmunt Bauman argues that modern relationships to place (physical, geographic, social) resemble the frailty of a tourist's connection to the places they go. The "presumption of temporariness" informs their outlook and behavior, so they make no "effort to construct a hard and tough frame of mutual rights and obligations and mutually binding rules of conduct" because, chances are, they won't see the same people again.[22] Bauman uses liquid matter as a metaphor to characterize the fluidity of modern culture and its institutions, the dissolution of the public commons, the shifting, temporariness of social relations, and the (consequential) vulnerability of the individual. By contrast, in solid modernity a person could retire from the same company where they were hired 30 years prior. Seeing the same people regularly around the office and neighborhood formed a connection and a commitment to those people. In other words, showing up was built into the way we lived our lives.

You could argue, and some scholars have, that the internet is a remediation of the commons or the public sphere, but the comparison is imprecise. While mobile internet technology has lowered barriers of entry and made some aspects of political organizing and information-sharing easier, "the same technologies that facilitate cooperation, connection, and community can also facilitate discord, anxiety and alienation."[23] Generally speaking, communication practices online do not support qualities hospitable to a robust and healthy public. By design, many social media platforms facilitate processes of exclusion more easily than processes of inclusion. The publicness, brevity, and replicability of communication online do not lend themselves to qualities like curiosity and tolerance or to the type of rational debate that helps create critically informed public opinion. Instead, new networked forms of association foster, at best, temporary and weak social bonds, which work to undermine and evaporate social trust. Not only that, but some digital infrastructures accelerate pernicious division, radicalization, racism, and hate.[24]

The very conditions of drift I have been describing—dislocation, fragmentation, filter bubbles, disconnection—are structural problems.

Addressing these problems requires individuals to look beyond the self and risk engaging with others. In doing so, they might recognize that this uncertain world is humanmade and that their personal experience of angst and precarity is common to others. However, systemic inequities cannot be fixed through individualized "biographical solutions.[25] To ameliorate public problems, we need to raise questions in public (whether on- or offline) about the institutions, structures, and social conditions that gave rise to those problems.[26]

I offer this book in response to current experiences of drift. The various contradictions, contingencies, and dualities that animate our lifeworld create a paradoxical sense of being both uprooted and mired. My (hopeful) argument is that this space—this disquieting, liminal space—is the space of potential action. The goal is to expand that space, to sit with its inherent discomforts, and make more room for unexpected spontaneous action. The examples I've included are born of that space. In other words, you can experience drift's spaciousness as emptiness or as fullness.

Facing Uncertainty

Even before contemporary sociologists labeled our tendency toward drift, ancient Greek philosophers described a similar source of human inhibition they called, akrasia. Akrasia is a troubling "weakness of will" characterized by the habit of not listening to what we accept should be heard and a failure to act on what we know is right.[27] Conceptually, akrasia accounts for the contradictory nature of human experience.

Not all ancient Greek philosophers were willing to accept this aspect of human nature. In fact, as some philosophers and classicists point out, Socrates the idealist, rejected the very idea of akrasia because he refused to believe that a person could act against her own principles.[28] By contrast, his student Plato was less staunch and recognized that, in some cases, humans would rather suppress their tendency toward conscientiousness to avoid the friction of public life.

Writing in the wake of the Peloponnesian war, Plato expressed hope through his fictional dialogue between Socrates and Adeimantus that philosophers would become moral leaders but worried that their akrastic tendencies would cause them to turn away from situations deemed hopeless. In Book IV of *The Republic*, Plato imagines how reasonable and justice-loving philosophers could feel like "travelers caught in a storm" fighting the temptation to "retreat behind a wall to shelter from the driving gusts of dust and hail." His apparent concern was that philosophers, "seeing the rest of the world full of iniquity," would withdraw from public life and just as soon "leave this world with a fair hope of the next."[29] Plato's millennia-old description of restlessness and personal disempowerment parallels my characterization of contemporary symptoms of drift.

Fortunately, the same ancient Greek philosophers who debated akrasia were unanimous in their recognition its near opposite—a human capacity for virtuous action in the face of uncertainty. *Phronesis*, as they called it, is a practical wisdom that guides a person to do the right thing in the right place, at the right time, in the right way, and for the right reason. According to Plato's student, Aristotle, a phronetic action responds to the particulars of a concrete reality while adhering to certain universal truths.[30]

In the twentieth century, pragmatic philosopher John Dewey broadened Aristotle's conception of phronesis to account for the world's irreducible complexity. He writes, "Aristotle acknowledges contingency, but he never surrenders his bias in favor of the fixed, certain and finished."[31] For Dewey, phronesis is a quality of attention, an attunement to the uncertainties within situations that demand a response and a sensitivity to the pressures affecting the context of concern. Psychologist Barry Schwartz invokes a jazz metaphor in his description of phronesis to highlight those same qualities of artful attunement, responsiveness, and improvisation.[32]

Other divergent theoretical treatments describe phronesis as either cognitive or performative, relying on specific, logic-based rules for decision making or on conventions of representation. In his work on *prudentia*, Cicero's Latin term for Aristotle's Greek phronesis, Robert Hariman argues that practical wisdom "requires implicit understanding of the possible, the probable, and the appropriate within a specific community."[33] Hariman's invocation of appropriateness echoes other theoretical treatments of phronesis, which suggest that norms, rules, and precedent govern correct action. From this perspective, phronetic action is hamstrung by formal reason, or doxastic logic. Yet phronesis is neither algorithm nor heuristic. It is a meta-rationality that exists at the intersection between what is practical and what is necessary.[34]

Over the years, humanities disciplines such as philosophy, classics and communication studies, have conceptually reworked phronesis but have yet to settle on a satisfactory theoretical treatment. With due reverence for its intellectual history, I humbly submit phronesis as the capacity to discern a practical course of action, one that preserves noble values, in unusual or complicated situations. Because of its entanglement in the contingent and the communal, phronesis eludes comprehensive description. Consensus is that phronetic qualities are best gleaned through case study, which is the approach this book takes. My goal is to add dimension to existing theorizations of phronesis by studying quotidian manifestations, particularly ones that highlight its creative, quirky, and even indecorous qualities. By emphasizing the contingency, versatility, and imperfection of rhetorical practice along with an insistence on intersectionality the case studies work to rehabilitate phronesis for the twenty-first century. If phronesis is the insight that precedes noble action in the public sphere, then this book is an archaeology of that insight.

When I first learned about phronesis, it sounded like a superpower. Imagine being able to say and do the right thing in any situation. But phronesis is not a superpower. It is not a mysterious talent possessed by a privileged few. Everyone has the capacity for phronesis.[35] Yet doing the right thing, as contemporary American philosopher Maxine Greene points out— "doesn't come automatically; it comes through being alive, awake, curious, and often furious."[36] Unlike akrasia, phronesis is a turning toward situations that appear hopeless.

Phronesis is a form of insight that acknowledges the essentially tragic structure of existence and compels us toward action anyway. It relies on a certain inquisitive quality of attention, a willingness to take risks, and a capacity for moral imagination. As poet/statesman Václav Havel wrote, "It is not the conviction that something will turn out well, but the certainty that something makes sense, regardless of how it turns out."[37] Sometimes, it requires seriously entertaining those first thoughts, the label Walt Whitman uses for those wild ideas unobstructed by social politeness and internal censor.[38] But the urge to act must also be tempered by a critical self-awareness of our own situation vis-à-vis others, and the power and privilege dynamics at play.

Knowing whether and how to act begins with a critical form of self-knowledge that, if done well, yields a careful blend of uniqueness and essentialism.[39] For philosopher Simone Weil, the process involves paying "a certain kind of attention" to the self in the world, a recognition that the self is inherently intersubjective—a formation dependent on the existence and care of unknown others.[40] It is about determining your location, positionality, and intersectionality, your fit within what Martin Luther King Jr. called the "network of mutuality."[41]

The language of intersectionality is a gift from Black feminist scholars, most notably legal scholar and civil rights advocate, Kimberlé Crenshaw, who experienced the limits of language's explanatory power when it came to understanding identity politics.[42] As a Black woman, Crenshaw saw herself at an intersection between binaries of race and gender. Intersectionality, then, became a way to talk about identity with more nuance and precision by visualizing a constellation of reciprocal vectors of race, gender, class, ethnicity, religion, ability, sexuality, and so on.[43]

Knowing yourself in this way means understanding your location and the conditions you take for granted as well as reflecting deeply on where you place your body and with whom you build affective ties.[44] A person who understands their intersectional fit who can identify contingencies in which they could positively affect change, and who has the courage to carry out public action, is a person ripening toward phronesis.

Embracing Strangerhood

We cannot keep avoiding our responsibilities to each other and to the planet. If we don't begin to imagine a blueprint for a more hospitable world, then we can expect more of the same—a collective experience of powerlessness, manifested in feelings of personal meaninglessness, loneliness, mistrust, insecurity, and anxiety.[45] Some scholars describe a form of world citizenship that seeks to transcend strangeness and abolish exclusion by widening identification with all of humanity; that is not necessarily what I am endorsing.[46] Transcendence is really hard. A better goal, for now, might be to make peace with our irreducible otherness and become engaged with strangers in our vicinity. That practice will open us up to cultivating a broader sense of responsibility for the fate of strangers in distress around the world.

To our benefit, strangerhood presumes an intersubjective, relational conception of the self. Strangerhood acknowledges coexistence with unknown and unfamiliar others. Strangers occupy an ambivalent social position, towing the line between insider and outsider. They resist easy categorization as friend or enemy. As such, strangers inspire curiosity. Curiosity could be a useful disposition in the context of a global diaspora; A curiosity that engages (rather than suppresses) difference through genuine dialogue and mutual exchange.[47] Unfortunately, our most public examples of encountering difference are found in commercial acts of pseudo-multiculturalism that rely on physical traits like race, gender, and ethnicity to fulfill some sort of superficial scorecard that perceives diversity as a product. These sorts of practices fetishize difference and can promote more harm than good.[48] And at the very least they miss out on opportunities for meaningful engagement. Still, my focus is on the productive ways people can live into the condition of mutual strangerhood. If we accept as a given our irreducible otherness, then we can begin to establish an ethics of reciprocal responsibility to live together as relative strangers.

Sociological scholars identify two primary types of *strangers*. The first type of stranger is the third person who helps solve disputes.[49] From this perspective, the stranger's value is her unique, outsider perspective. The second type of stranger is a person on the margin—migrants, newcomers, visitors, or guests who struggle to be socially accepted by the locals.[50] This stranger seeks inclusion into the main group. Liquid modernity's climate of contingency, mobility, and hyper-individualism primes many of us to relate to the second type of stranger, as we struggle to find our fit, footing, and value.

To feel empowered to act in conditions of liquidity, we must adopt and adapt qualities associated with both types of strangers. Recall the first type of stranger, who occupies an esteemed position by her ability to resolve local disputes. She has been socialized elsewhere, so she sees the constructed nature of the local social order. Her outsider vision enables her to offer an alternative path forward. This stranger relies on her own background and subjectivity, whether a formal area of expertise or her own lived experiences, to guide her insight. Yet her temporary role as referee does not commit her to the locality. She risks becoming one of Bauman's tourists who arrives one day and leaves the next. The other type of stranger sees her background as the cost for belonging. She tries to assimilate into the local culture but is never fully welcomed. Like the third-party stranger, she can see the constructed nature of the social order, but she maintains a level of respect for the locals' conventional way of doing things. She values the locality and its inherent potential for community. The danger for this stranger is that, in her effort to fit in, she becomes estranged from herself.[51] Neither form of strangerhood is ideal, yet an amalgam of the two—someone who exhibits self-assuredness in their strangeness *and* maintains reverence for locality and its contingencies—might be a useful prototype. This is the orientation that potentiates phronesis.

The people featured in this book demonstrate this dual quality of strangerhood. None of them are originally from the places they inhabit. They are outsiders to both the locality and the conflicts in which they engage. They make use of this positionality through practical acts of creativity and imagination. They begin with a relational, critical understanding of the self.[52] Based on their interview responses, they seem to recognize themselves as strangers in a strange world and accept, without judgment, their own merits and limitations. Philosopher Iris Murdoch describes this positioning activity as *unselfing*. For Murdoch, goodness is an attempt to unself and "join the world as it really is." Goodness, she argues, is a function of the will achieved through embodied action. "Nothing counts as an act," according to Murdoch, unless it brings about "a recognizable change in the world."[53] Thus, good action is born of a certain level of discernment that clarifies when it's worthwhile to struggle against injustice and when it's better to devote oneself to private projects of self-creation. To me, Murdoch is writing about something akin to phronesis with her emphasis on discernment and good public action.

A goal in writing this book is to pull back the curtain on phronesis. I wanted to know how some people were able to stake their footing and carry out unexampled acts of goodness. That was the central question in all my interviews—"how did you do it?" The book you are holding represents a composite answer. In it, the stories I share offer examples of what it means to show up as a stranger for strangers in strange times. The people and the contexts you will read about are distinct yet they're all doing a version of the same thing. They slow down long enough to notice a problem, identify whether and how they could be of benefit, and then they risk action.

Enacting Practical Wisdom

This book takes a deep dive into the phronetic process by examining creative and beneficent ways ordinary people have responded to social, political, and economic problems in their areas. None of the people in this book participate in a movement or in organized, collectivized action. Rather they act independently, and in response to the specifics of their unique context. You will learn how Israeli and Palestinian environmentalists negotiate water politics in the Jordan River basin, how artists support the resettlement of refugees, how sewing centers create jobs for populations prone to human trafficking, how volunteers turn unused lots into edible landscapes, and how US war veterans connect Afghan saffron farmers to the global market. Each featured account offers a snapshot of catalytic moments and initial attempts as well as a descriptive account of what things look like on the ground now. Rather than assembling each account into a cohesive narrative, I present them one at a time in standalone chapters. Presenting the stories this way honors their complexity and individuality.

Although each person acts independently, there is something altogether familiar about them, a common ethic you could call contemporary phronesis, or you might also just call showing up. In the context of drift and uncertainty, the people in this book show up. They exalt the space between dualities, the space between impossible and possible, individual, and collective, contextual, and universal, insider and stranger. From this liminal space, they open up possibilities for action. They maintain fidelity to universal values even as they transgress societal ones. Often, the wisdom in their action links to its inherent subversiveness.

The most practical thing to do is not always the most rational. As a result, what each person does seems revolutionary but, in truth, their approaches are not especially difficult or complex. Nor are their interventions large-scale or extraordinary. To be sure, they are out-of-the ordinary, but they are relatively small in scale and grounded in a mundane sense of the local. Working together in this way—showing up for one another—is how we can expand our individual and collective capacities to act.

Throughout this book you will likely identify recurrent themes—how fear can be an indicator of areas for growth, how impermanence gives permission to take risks, or how the accumulation of your lived experience has real value in the world. You might even sketch out some sort of operative moral code associated with honesty, generosity, care for the environment, and respect for human dignity. The theoretical framework that I have developed in this introduction attempts to make sense of all these—strangers enacting phronesis among strangers. I titled each of the chapters that follow using verbs I consider relevant to the particular story, and ones that seem to enable phronesis. They are not mutually exclusive. Nor are they hierarchical or linear. Rather, they are compatible and congruent. In fact, sometimes I found myself hard pressed to decide which verb to assign which story because all the stories reflect elements of each. I invite you to disagree, compare and contrast, and find verbs you think are key to phronetic action. At the end of each chapter, I reflect on the thematic verb, connect ideas, extend patterns, and preview the next chapter. The book closes with a final meditation that absorbs the main takeaways and considers how you might enact practical wisdom in your own life to get you going on your peace path.

Thinking back to the summer of 2018 when I first conceived this project, it wasn't the litany of problems but the thinness of our connection that heavied my heart. I worried that, like me, others with the impulse to do good would lack inspiration, imagination, and social courage. I wanted to offer precedent. In her book, *Braiding Sweetgrass*, Robin Wall Kimmerer recounts administering a survey to students in her General Ecology class that asked them to rate their knowledge of positive interactions between humans and the land. Their survey responses averaged zero. She writes, "I was stunned. How is it possible that in twenty years of education they cannot think of any beneficial relationships between people and the environment? Perhaps the negative examples they see every day—brown fields, factory farms, suburban sprawl—truncated their ability to see some good between humans and the earth."[54] A lack of story or, more precisely, the presence of a detrimental story truncated their ability to see. The stories we tell ourselves draw a thin line between agency and victimhood, between phronesis and akrasia.

I read once, in an early childhood development book, that a sense of security is nothing more than an expectation for goodness. Or as the authors put it, "confidence and trust in the goodness of me, you, us."[55] Caregivers cultivate an expectation for goodness through consistent open-hearted care and attentiveness. It strikes me that the ecology students in Kimmerer's class have little expectation for positive human interaction with the earth. Their sense of resignation sounds like my own students who report to me with startling fatalism what it is like to go to school after a mass shooting or participate in active shooter training while adults debate the merits of gun regulation. I fear we are letting our young people down by leaving them defenseless. They are justifiably losing an expectation for goodness and, with it, a secure attachment to the world. I am writing this book with the hope that it provides reassurance, grants permission, offers precedent, and inspires action.

ONE

Trust Your Partners

Just be a citizen of your community—
be aware and give as much as you take.

—SHAWN LENT

From the sitting area by the entrance to the dance studio, I watched Shawn Lent finish teaching a private ballet class. Her pupil was a statuesque young woman around the age of seventeen who glided across the wood parquet floor to the tinkling of piano music. Lent circled her as she danced, directing cues to her reflection in the mirror. "Thumbs in! Two more. Travel, travel! Squeeze from the back. Open up! Back foot is the driver. Better, better! Even more! Yes! Feel the difference?" From what I could glimpse of her face in the mirror, the young woman looked unfazed, effortlessly incorporating Lent's instructions as she continued with a series of dizzying piqué turns. When the song ended, the dancer finished in plié. Lent gave instructions for what to practice at home.

While all this was going on, younger girls between ages seven and twelve began filing into the studio. Their mothers, who wore hijabs, took seats in the waiting area. Lent's assistant, a young woman in her twenties, helped the girls get changed into tights and leotards. It was clear they were new to dance. One of them came out of the dressing room with her leotard on backwards. Lent's assistant lowered her chin and whispered to the little girl who smiled sheepishly and retreated to the dressing room. Some mothers stayed to watch, others left and would return at the end of the hour-long class.

The girls were refugees from Syria, Iraq, and Myanmar (formerly known as Burma). They were there to rehearse "Waltz of the Flowers" for their upcoming performance in *The Nutcracker*. Lent's demeanor changed noticeably as she welcomed the children. She has been a dancer her entire life so her posture was still bolt upright as she floated across the floor to greet them, but her compact muscles loosened. Her attitude became jovial, even goofy. She made exaggerated faces and affected cartoonish voices as she led the dancers through a seated stretching routine in a circle on the floor. Lent has been offering free weekly dance classes to refugee children in Chicago since 2016. As much as it's about dancing, it's also about settling into a new city.

Lent described her initiative, Dance Peace, as a neighborhood project. It's not an act of charity or a therapeutic intervention. It's about fellowship and community. "A lot of people ask me if we're doing dances where they can express their stories and talk about the trauma," said Lent. She continued:

> I mean, they've witnessed—we had people witness their father dying. One girl has lived in five countries in five years and wasn't able to do anything on the left and we got her doing actual cross lateral patterning. So, some of it is like *physical* therapy, but we don't do therapy work. I partner and do referrals with dance movement therapists who are working with refugee populations, but for this group, what I've noticed is that they are *just so* still in this.

That is, in part, why Lent keeps the mood light during these classes. "Bringing some joy is really important for this group in particular. I have other groups that are not taking it seriously, and this group walks in like—*serious,*" she said furrowing her brow to emphasize the word.

Their seriousness reflects the heaviness of events in their homelands. In Syria, civil war broke out in 2011 as part of the wider Arab Spring protests in opposition to President Bashar Al-Assad.[1] In Iraq, central political institutions crumbled as a consequence of war, conquest, revolution or a combination of the three.[2] And in Myanmar, members of the majority Buddhist population have used violence and intimidation to remove the Rohingya, a Muslim minority group. Thousands of Rohingya have been murdered and their homes and mosques destroyed.[3]

DURING THE DANCE CLASS that I observed, I noticed how Lent referred to the children as dancers, never students or kids. In a way, she was calling them into being, a process aided by the donning of a costume. It is important that every child who walks through the door transforms into a dancer, beginning with the proper attire. "We have no funds for any of that but were able to secure tons of donations. . . . Anyone who walks in, we can usually find something. But that is really important," explained Lent. During the first year of the program, she couldn't offer costumes. And once she did, she noticed a shift. She described it as a level of respect, self-respect. The dancers felt that the people around them were taking them and their dancing seriously. Each dancer receives tights, skirts, slippers, and leotards to take home. They become responsible for them, which creates a sense of ownership and belonging. Besides, the girls and their mothers visibly brightened when they came out of the dressing room in ballerina garb.

Like the costumes, the weekly dance classes are free of charge. For tax purposes Lent named her initiative Dance Peace, but is adamant that it remains an open-ended community-led program rather than a mission-based nonprofit organization. She does not want to impose a set of values or presume community needs. Rather she wants to remain open and responsive to community feedback and needs as they arise. She keeps her goal simple— to welcome refugees to the neighborhood and help them integrate easefully. "We've had a few small grants for performances, but we have all donated equipment, all donated stuff, donated staff time, my time, so it's like. It's very community-led," explained Lent. Because it is community-led, the program's offerings change to reflect whoever is participating. For a few years the children took music classes because a musician offered to teach. Teenagers and young adults who study dance, like Lent's assistant, volunteer as a way to practice developing and teaching choreography.

> We have volunteer drivers, translators, if any of the parents or staff asked us to go to their things, we go to their things. We go to their lessons, we go to their cultural activities, we go to their protests, we go to their demonstrations, we go to their house for birthday parties. When the landlord turns off the heat, we work with their case managers. It became an all-inclusive, comprehensive thing.

Dance Peace is essentially a neighborhood that is not geographically or linguistically bound. Rather, it is held together by a set of practices that reinforce membership and trust. As Lent explained, there is typically one parent per language who facilitates the phone tree.

> So, each of the communities—we have an Iraqi group, we have a northwestern African contingent, we have an Arab Syrian contingent, the Rohingya Burmese community [we have] at least one kind of parent or case manager in each of those who helps not only get the word out,

but also when there's changes, or who needs to have a women-only audience, all of those things.

Lent told me a few stories about how the community's interdependency saved the day. In one case she was driving around the city picking up donated costumes. It was raining, she got caught behind a train, and there was no way she would make it back to the studio in time for rehearsal. But then she remembered thinking, "'Wait! I don't have to cancel. Someone's got the key!' We had an engineering PhD student who had been watching class and he's like, 'I know the dance!' And he just led it and the parents led it and it was fine."

The ability to rely on others has not only been a necessity, but it has also been deeply fulfilling. Every year, the dancers perform at the mall and parents sew the costumes and do the decorations. "We have enough people that someone can have a bad day," said Lent. "There's room for that . . . and you can tell when a mom just really needs the time off, you know?" Lent's hope is that this network will carry on whether she continues offering dance classes, or not.

For Lent, community is not a metaphor. It is a felt reality, one that is tethered by responsibility, obligation, and integrity. Folklorist Burt Feintuch has observed that community is increasingly overused and under conceptualized, placing it in the same category as words like authenticity or tradition.[4] Today, it is not uncommon to hear a classroom or even a fitness studio describe itself as a community. But community must be more than a temporary network of shared interests in a particular time. Community is sustained through practice. It is a social imaginary realized and materialized through quotidian acts of caring—picking up a carton of milk, giving a ride to the airport, watching the kids, or attending a graduation party. What is unique about Lent's community is that it exists amid social tension.

THE DANCE STUDIO is in West Rogers Park in Chicago's oldest Jewish neighborhood, colloquially known as the golden ghetto, home to the Midwest's largest Jewish and Hasidic community. The neighborhood has recently diversified to include Indian, Pakistani, Bangladeshi, Russian, and Assyrian immigrant communities. As I walked from my hotel along the main commercial thoroughfare, Devon Street, I passed kosher bakeries, kebab houses, and halal restaurants. I saw every manner of headdress—baseball caps, yarmulkes, and hijabs. Yet, despite their proximity to one another, the cultural groups rarely interact. Each has its own grocery store, school, library, and, in some cases, 9–1–1 service. Lent talked about a young woman, one of her dance students, from the Hasidic Orthodox Jewish neighborhood who was about to leave for Tel Aviv University. She had never made an Arab friend. "Their lives are so insular," said Lent.

The one place these groups share, however, is the performing arts center where Lent teaches her dance classes. She noticed that both her Jewish and Arab students signed up for classes on Sundays. "It's the day they have in common," she said, referring to the fact that Muslims worship Fridays and Jews worship Saturdays. Lent remembered having an epiphany, "I'm already embedded in the Orthodox and Hasidic community, so it was great to do something I was already doing. I'm already getting paid to teach here. Why don't I just open it up and have a free class for the refugee community?" And so, she did.

> We did like six months with no funding whatsoever. Just all volunteer. Myself volunteer, everything volunteer. The kids performed through the Syrian community [. . .] they had a big picnic and that was—it felt very successful. No costumes or anything, you know, and then we were able to get a few costumes, which is good and they danced in the re- cital. And once I noticed what was happening at the recital—the pride in the whole family, and also you could tell the other families are like, "What's happening?" because there's usually not a lot of hijabs ever in dance studios.

A flashbulb went off in Lent's head. "I was like, 'Oh, we got to integrate them into classes!'" She worked with the studio to get a low enough rate so that the refugee children could attend other dance classes throughout the day, not just the free one she offered. "Having people in hijabs come in and out of the studio, just as a common thing, I mean *that* was the first big change," said Lent, "and also changing the schedule to realize both Jew- ish and Muslim holidays—those kinds of things." These small-scale, habit- forming changes helped to kindle a cross-cultural sense of community.

However, integration is more complicated than assembling diverse bod- ies into a shared dance class. Lent knew she couldn't just treat refugee stu- dents like all the other students. "Right now, they need a direct contact," she explained. "They need translation in four different languages. They need personal support to get to that place of equity. We're not there yet," she said. She listed some of the ways refugee families need accommodation such as taking extra care to communicate class schedules and upcoming events. "You just need to tell them when they come. You can't send them the full schedule. They're not able to really decipher those things yet, and besides those personal contacts show they are welcome. It takes a couple of years for [frictionless integration] to happen." Still, Lent began to notice some early signs of progress.

Her dancers perform three recitals annually, each increasing in scope. They do a small show for the refugee community at a potluck or picnic, followed by a recital at the mall, and then finally a large-scale public performance of *The Nutcracker*. Lent was quick to acknowledge that *The Nutcracker* is an ironic choice. "It's so problematic, it's hilarious," she laughed. The reason they do it, though, is because *The Nutcracker* is iconic. Everyone knows it, so it is a useful place to begin building something together. Folklore scholars have long argued that folk performances foster mutual identification and the creation of a shared identity.[5] Lent smiled and playfully suppressed an eye roll as she said:

> Everybody loves it! It's so problematic. Like the Christmas party—so first of all, most of our students are Muslim [laughs] and then we have our Jewish friends and they're all at a Christmas party. And then there's all these ethno-stereotypes in the second half. But we've been—I've been—really proud of this community production. We work with Chinese exchange students to do the Chinese number [. . .] with Flamenco dancers to do a traditional Spanish dance. One year the senior center's belly dance club did the Arabic part [. . .].

Another reason *The Nutcracker* works for the large community production is because it carries a sense of prestige. Lent described a palpable pride among children and parents when it comes to their participation in *The Nutcracker*. "We work with that," said Lent. So even if it is not an ideal production, *The Nutcracker* fits the bill.

Working cross-culturally makes it difficult to know what is appropriate all the time. Lent said she has made mistakes—saying or doing the wrong things—but grounds herself through regular, active reflection. "We each have moments, you know, and I always question, like, why am I teaching these kids this white dance, this westernized ballet?" The process of critical reflection forces Lent to reconcile the raced and gendered aspects of ballet. Through her questioning she decided that the advantages of ballet outweigh the problems.

> It's a great place to start because everybody knows what it is, or they think they know. There's a comfort and there's a confidence in knowing

what ballet is. If I throw other things, then they actually back off, right? So, sometimes it might appear like I am the white lady in the front from America and I'm teaching you in a row. [. . .] There are sometimes where it's appropriate for who's in the room, but it might not be appropriate for someone who's just walking in, and then sometimes that's the opposite, right? So, I think I've made mistakes, you know, but usually it's always collaborative, close-knit.

Lent's approach to Dance Peace has been a lot like dancing itself. With refugee families as her partners, she has been open, responsive, and rhythmic, communicating directly from body to body using gestures that signify emotional states. Even as missteps happen, the partners remain in dialogue, allowing the dance to be driven by context.

The buzzing auditorium after the first *Nutcracker* performance was a clear sign that Lent's humility and context-based approach was working. After the show, she went to look for one of the refugee mothers who had been instrumental in tailoring the costumes.

It's funny, I went to say thank you to the mother and her friends, could not find them anywhere! Just so integrated in the auditorium, that I couldn't even find anybody because everybody was really mixed and mingled. So, there's moments where [. . .] you can see it in physical presence. In the dancers it's just being comfortable trusting your own body, then trusting sitting at a table with people, you know, being able to sit, to look someone in the eye, to share the sidewalk, to share the lobby.

Audience has been key to Dance Peace's success. Audience plays a role in any performance by mentally mirroring the emotional states they see on stage. For Dance Peace, the role of the audience is even more critical because participating as an audience member in a diverse group flattens cultural differences and creates mutual identification. The simple act of sitting in the same room watching the same performances creates identification through embodiment, or con-sensus; the word from Latin meaning shared feeling. Moreover, the presence of an audience and their attention uplifts the dancers and supports their self-esteem.

Lent's idea of dancing as a way to welcome refugee families was not unfounded. She had a set of formative experiences that guided her on the path. In college she studied choreography. She danced professionally for two years afterward but gave it up to pursue opportunities in social justice work.

In 2001 she received a ministry visa to go and work in a Muslim community in East London. She expected her job to involve church-based arts programming. Her first day of work was September 9th, two days before the fateful attacks. She said on September 11th, "everything shifted."

> It's all an immigrant neighborhood. I'm the only American there, supposed to be converting people to Christianity. I'm on an Evangelical Christian mission in an all-Muslim neighborhood. There were some Sikh families as well, I didn't even know what Sikhism is, like, I'd never been to a mosque before. And 9/11 was my second day of work there, and I was working with young men mostly in and out of the juvenile justice system. These are young men ages 18 to 22 who are from immigrant Muslim families. So, there were questions of radicalization, what are they learning in the mosque, their mosques were raided for connections to Saudi—so that was intense.

As a young woman in her mid-twenties with a background in dance, she did what she knew best. She danced, and she taught the young Muslim men to dance, and she taught them about American football. "I didn't convert anybody," she smiled, "but I really learned about diplomacy through dance." She stayed for three years; the experience was so transformative that it propelled her to graduate school where she would study dance as a form of social intervention.

In 2012 she received a Fulbright scholarship to explore the role of artist-as-catalyst for social change in Egypt. Upon her arrival, however, the program was suspended because of the increasingly violent uprisings against then-President Mohamed Morsi.[6] Lent was able to stay in Egypt on a technicality and worked for the US embassy where she helped students, scholars, and artists prepare for their trip to the United States.

> There were a lot of refugees, because a lot of embassies were closed in the Middle East—Gaza, Yemen, Syria. They all are coming through Cairo to get all their paperwork to go to the US. So, I met a lot of Syrian refugees, met a lot of Yemeni refugees and some were like [. . .] "I'm going to Chicago," and I was like, "Oh that's where I used to live and am probably going back."

She did go back eventually, four years later, with an Egyptian man she met and married while she was there. Upon her return to Chicago in 2016, Lent was met with one of the nation's most memorable Presidential election campaigns. "We came back, like were filing the paperwork almost the same day as Trump did the like, 'we will ban all Muslim immigrants,'" she re-called, shaking her head. The day after the election, Lent remembers feeling stunned and described where she was in the city when she first learned about Trump's victory.

> There's this beautiful statue on the other side of the river—it's from World War II, and it's to show that even since the first days of this country, it's been inter-religious. So, it's [. . .] a sculpture of George Washington and his two Jewish advisors. And then it's got a wonderful plaque about diversity and what is the United States. And then on the back side of it is this relief work. It's a long panel and it's just the Statue of Liberty, doing this welcome gesture, like arms fully outstretched and people running to her from all over the world. It's this marble sort of thing, and it faces Trump Tower, so I was standing next to the sculpture that says all this stuff in image and word facing the giant Trump name, and I just started dancing. And then people started joining, and then we had a series of protests in the city.

When I asked her about her impulse to dance on the day after Trump's surprise win, she said that her body needed to release something. "Other people feel it in their bodies too. That tension—it's because you're passion-ate and usually so passionate—there's a reason you march. It's in your body. You gotta either take space or express it in some way," she said.

AS LENT RESETTLED BACK HOME in Chicago, she met some of the refugees who she had worked with in Egypt. They were looking for volunteer opportu-nities that would help improve their English-speaking confidence. Some were participating in an organization called Syrian Community Network. Lent recommended dance. It would not only help with their English, but also as she explained, "with their own trust, the use of space, the idea of taking up space, being applauded by your peers, being applauded by other families." Dance would help their confidence, in general. So, she started of-fering dance classes for children and gave plenty of opportunities for adults to volunteer. "When people see the word 'refugee,' they're just like, 'Oh I want to help. I'll give you this,'" remarked Lent. Rarely do they ask what refugees can contribute to the community. This one-way dynamic frustrates Lent. Part of her project has been to flip the script on what helping entails.

> They're artists, they can sew, they are music teachers, they are leaders [. . .] one girl started a whole youth group for positive action, they're

leaders. What are their contributions? What are they bringing that's exciting, you know? So, I'm hoping to get just more of that from the community and it's already starting a little bit [. . .] like, what do you bring? What do you give?

The opportunity to contribute creates a feeling of agency and belonging. Most people do not want to be seen as charity cases and refugees are no different. "We always talk about outreach and all this like we're somewhere else," said Lent incredulously. She powered on:

> Look at your own neighborhood [. . .] figure out how your contribution helps and doesn't compete, or harm, or duplicate efforts. But also [. . .] take those resources too. I take a stepping class and a painting class from the elders at the public housing. I'm also a student of my community, learning from them, taking a step back, asking so many questions, asking them to step up [. . .] not using people but finding resources so they are paid or have some benefit, but help make a healthier ecosystem. You know? Just be a citizen of your community—be aware and give as much as you take.

Giving and taking. Stepping back and leaning in. It is hard to ignore the dance metaphor that supports Lent's outlook toward community. And as a lifelong dancer, she responds with grace and finesse. In partner dancing, learning to follow is a skill that requires improvisation and split-second interpretation of things that are almost never perfect. There was no way for Lent to predict what moves were coming next—September 11th, the Arab Spring, and President Trump—but through all of it, she managed to keep her balance, and maintain connection, squeezing from the back and opening up to the world.

Reflection

Lent's story draws out the ways in which phronesis is like a dance. She created community from displacement by establishing and practicing trust. She established trust through her responsiveness, sensitivity, and consistency of action. She practiced trust by letting go through delegation and self-reflection. I will expound on these qualities as I see them in Lent's story, but first I want to introduce another ancient Greek concept, kairos, that will allow us to consider the role of timing and timeliness regarding practical wisdom.

Kairos translates as the right time, or an opportune moment. Some understandings of kairos attach it to God or Spirit to convey its mysterious qualities. Serendipity is kairotic, for example. Many of the stories in this book reflect an element of kairos. Be on the lookout for them. In Lent's case, she describes experiencing an "epiphany" when she noticed that her Jewish and Arab students were signing up for classes on Sundays. She also describes a "flashbulb" going off after the first recital when she saw the value of audience integration. Even though Lent makes it sound simple, it would be unfair and inaccurate to only give credit to kairos.

Timing is not all there is to it; Lent had been primed for receiving and recognizing kairos. Recall, she studied dance as a form of social intervention in graduate school, so she was already attuned in that regard. On top of that, she practiced a quality of attention that allowed her to notice a pattern in the scheduling requests as well as the sensitivity and willingness to respond to those requests by opening the studio on Sundays and then by working with the studio to get a low enough rate so refugee children could attend other dances classes beyond the free one she offered. Lent's perception and receptivity correlate to the broader ethic of trust I mentioned above. She trusts her partners implicitly and demonstrates a flexible, responsiveness in her engagement with them.

From the start, she did not presume the needs of her refugee neighbors. She kept her goal broad and simple—to welcome refugees to the community and help them integrate more easily. Along the way, she admits to missteps ("So, I think I've made mistakes, you know, but usually it's always collaborative, close-knit."), she acknowledges limitations ("I always question, like, why am I teaching these kids this white dance, this westernized ballet?"), and she demonstrates the agility required to handle problems as they arise ("'Wait! I don't have to cancel. Someone's got the key!'"). Phronesis relies on the ability to remain nimble. Like dance, it requires practice. Lent has patience and discipline on her side. She also demonstrates humility in a variety of ways (admitting mistakes, active self-reflection, and self-questioning), as well as in her stated resistance to forming a nonprofit.

Lent told me her hope is for Dance Peace, or some version of it, to continue regardless of her participation. She wants a self-sustaining community of care, not a mission-driven nonprofit. Lent consistently emphasizes the community and her partners ("We've had a few small grants for performances, but we have all donated equipment, all donated stuff, donated staff time, my time, so it's like—it's very community-led."). It is this lack of self-importance, this humility, that prevents Lent from drawing the essence of her creation into the personal ego.

The next chapter, "Know Your Limits," builds on the themes of responsiveness, humility, and delegation, as well as the practice of self-scrutiny. The person you meet, Curtis Romjue, is devoutly curious. You will notice how his constant questioning leads him to live, as poet Rainer Maria Rilke writes, in ever "widening circles."[7] Contrary to this chapter, the next one will feature a nonprofit organization, but like Dance Peace, the mission remains broad enough to allow for contingency, movement, and redirection.

TWO

Know Your Limits

Chill out! Take comfort in your smallness.

—CURTIS ROMJUE

I met Curtis Romjue over Memorial Day Weekend in 2019 at his office in the Ballard District of Seattle, Washington. When I first pulled up to the address he gave me, I hesitated to turn off my car. It didn't look like an office building. It looked like an old Victorian mansion. I let the car idle while I double-checked my map. This was right. I shut off the engine and popped open the door with my elbow. Just then, an enormous black raven alighted on the building's peak. According to Indigenous peoples of the Pacific Northwest coast of North America, the raven symbolizes curiosity and mischief and is a source of light, and transformation. I took it as a sign I was in the right place.

Ballard was not what I expected of Seattle and, as I learned after talking to Romjue and some other locals, Ballard doesn't really consider itself part of Seattle anyway. Seattle proper never wanted it. In fact, after years of staunch refusal, the city had to forcibly incorporate Ballard in 1907. The area never lost its anti-conformist attitude. The Ballard district is based around the Salmon Bay fishing industry and the locals consist of a quirky mix ranging from grizzled Scandinavian fishermen to young urban hipsters. From his appearance, Romjue fell somewhere between the two. He was young— mid-thirties with a fresh face and Peter Pan-like features. He wore a fisherman's beanie and a collared, short sleeve, button up shirt with whales on it. His face lit up as I approached, and he immediately made me feel welcome. He peppered me with questions as we ascended the well-worn staircase to his office. Where did I come from? How long had I been there? What did I like to do for fun? I was struck by how attentive he was to my brief, distracted responses. I felt his kind eyes watching my face as my researcher mind tried to take in all the details and my right hand scrambled for a rogue pen at the bottom of my shoulder bag. When we reached his office, he offered to make me tea and I accepted. It gave me a chance to find my pen and look around.

We were on the mansion's third floor in an attic-type space with dormered ceilings on either side of a window. I thought about the raven perched above our heads. The room felt like a cozy little nest, a raven's nest, with all kinds of worldly trinkets and treasures, collected not bought. The walls held posters and photographs. A guitar stood propped on a stand in the corner. Any available bookshelf or ledge made a home for a happy-looking house plant. When the electric kettle on a shelf began to hiss, Romjue produced a box of mixed tea bags and had me choose. I picked a spicy chai and took a seat at the little table in front of the window. It was the only place for us to sit together, really.

Romjue brought over the mugs of tea and took a seat opposite me at the table. Dust particles suspended in the air between us, reflecting the sun's rays and taking on the appearance of pixie dust. He knew I was there to learn about his nonprofit First Aid Arts, but as we sipped our tea we indulged in personal small talk. He spoke glowingly about his wife and two daughters. He shared photos and plans for upcoming family trips. There was such a kindness about him that I found myself feeling suspicious. He can't possibly be like this *all* the time; Can he? A shameful thought, I know. Yet after talking with him for a couple of hours and learning his story, I have to say I think he *is* like that all the time.

ROMJUE WAS A COLLEGE STUDENT studying philosophy at Seattle Pacific University when he first learned about modern slavery and human trafficking. He was at a lecture by Gary Haugen, a lawyer and the founding president of International Justice Mission, a nongovernmental organization (NGO) that focuses on human rights and law enforcement. Romjue left the lecture feeling shaken by what he learned and also a little bit embarrassed that he hadn't really known about it sooner. Looking back, he said it was the perfect time for him to have such an experience:

> As a college student where you're picking all of your classes and you have kind of, what can also be sort of the moment of like, the oppression of opportunity, you know? It's like you feel all the weight of—What should I do? What can I be? Who am I? You know, just kind of the existential crisis of that moment when you're not growing up

in a culture where it's like, your dad makes shoes and then you make shoes and it's all settled for you. Ironically having all the resources can sometimes—opportunity without purpose and without a sense of how to root your dignity and where your worth comes from—can lead to tragedy for some people.

The lecture by Haugen prompted Romjue to reflect on what he cared about, what he loved to do, and what he had to offer the world. Since childhood, he saw himself primarily as a musician. Some of his earliest memories involve dancing in the basement on the family's deep freezer, which he used as a makeshift stage for his tributes to Michael Jackson. After he heard Haugen speak, he remembered asking himself, "How can I help? I don't have money to give, I'm not a lawyer or a police officer. So, what does it look like for me to show up?" As a musician, Romjue did what he loved. He made music.

He already had a band, so he registered it as a 501c3 non-profit rock band, the first of its kind. "We were called Jubilee, and we used our music to raise awareness to fight human trafficking," he said. The band played at cafes, weddings, bar mitzvahs, and bars. Their playlist consisted of a lot of American indie rock—The Shins, Vampire Weekend, and Death Cab for Cutie. At gigs, they tried to take a subtle approach with regard to human trafficking. They didn't mention it outright between songs, but they let audiences know that part of their booking fee and sales from CDs would go to the International Justice Mission (IJM). Romjue smiled, "We wouldn't, at a wedding reception, say, 'Hey did you know that slavery still exists and like, while you're enjoying your feast here, people are dying.' We, you know, tried to be classy and tactful and appropriate," he explained.

Over the next five years, the band became increasingly popular. They were doing fewer covers and more of their own music. They played all over the city at hip bars and taverns like Neumos, The Triple Door, and the Tractor Tavern, or, as Romjue said with a chuckle, "places that typically you're not hearing about slavery." He told me about a time when he was playing at a bar, and someone left $500 in the band's tip jar. He also performed for Governor Gregoire a couple times and had the chance to bend her ear toward his cause.[1]

Romjue said he thought the reason music worked as opposed to other forms of communication is because music is sensory, shared, and distinctly human. He described people as having "spam filters in their brains" for the deluge of marketing pitches they hear on a daily basis. Music, he found, cuts through the noise.

When you hear somebody share from more of their humanity than just like their brain or a marketing pitch, when there's the emotion—think about Billie Holiday's voice or Martin Luther King Jr., the way that he spoke was so soulful and passionate that it was not just like ones and zeros in code or a message to be blocked out [. . .]—you can't fake that. That's the X factor, when someone's singing something and it's really felt and coming with [. . .] genuine conviction, that's something that gets people's attention.

Music enables a particular form of truth-telling. Singing or speaking from the heart projects a sincere vulnerability that is hard to ignore. As Romjue referenced, when Billie Holiday leveled the haunting lyrics of "Strange Fruit" at her audiences in the 1950s, she was conveying the brutal truth of the American South and the racial terror inflicted on Black people there every day.[2] Romjue reveres this form of consciousness-raising and he felt like he and his band were making traction around Seattle. Still, he wondered what else he could do to get more directly involved.

ONE DAY, by random chance, Romjue ran into Haugen at Dallas airport. He told Haugen about seeing his lecture and starting his band, and that he wanted to continue supporting IJM in a more direct way. Haugen connected Romjue with some members of the organization and Romjue became one of the first participants in a pilot program to train volunteers. He traveled to IJM's headquarters in Washington D.C. and, on a grant, went to Guatemala City so he could see their work firsthand. Guatemala, a beautiful place, is a dangerous one to be a young girl. The *Washington Post,* citing a UNICEF report, stated that in 2013, over three thousand girls between the ages of 10 and 14 were giving birth as a result of rape.[3]

Romjue's trip to Guatemala was eye-opening. He saw how a long history of civil war and political unrest created widespread poverty, child malnutrition, and violence. He met young victims of sexual violence, forced labor, and trafficking. He learned the story of inadequate government support, lack of public services, institutional failings, and poverty-driven desperation. He also observed the limitations of IJM, the organization that brought him there. Their work was important, he had no doubts about that. Haugen is a Harvard-trained lawyer who led the United Nations Rwanda genocide investigation, after all. Still, Romjue found himself wondering about what happens to the people after they are freed from violence and suffering. He began to formulate broader questions about the ethical implications of intervention.

> If you really want sustainable emancipation, you can't just knock a door down and grab someone from the situation. They need holistic care because they have trauma bonding, there's Stockholm Syndrome, [they may have] been addicted to drugs, their sense of self-worth and their world, like, they've been conditioned to believe that they can't see another identity or another life for themselves.

He said he had heard about girls returning to their oppressors and of perpetrators of violence threatening victims by telling them that their family will be harmed if they don't comply. Ever the philosophy major, Romjue began debating distinctions between rescue, relief, and restoration. He questioned the definition of justice, the role of power, and what other intervention processes could look like.

When he got home, he started exploring best practices in aftercare. He didn't know aftercare was the word for it at the time, but he was curious about how organizations support people who have been rescued from rice mills, brick kilns, and brothels. He wrote to a friend working in Uganda with children who were taken by the Lord's Resistance Army. She went there after she completed her graduate degree in counseling. Romjue asked how the kids were responding to therapy treatment. In her response, she sounded frustrated. He remembers the letter reading something like, "I'm here, I'm here to help them, I'm a counselor, but I can't do talk therapy with them until they'll talk to me, and the kids just won't talk to me." Her letter went on to describe an impromptu tactic that finally broke through and sort of worked to her amazement. She explained in her letter to Romjue that she wanted the children to relax, so she kicked a soccer ball around with them. Then she brought in some art supplies. All she had were markers and paper. Romjue recalled the letter:

> She described how the kids would draw what they couldn't say. So, she was just sharing how it's amazing, these kids are drawing, you know, what they can't [say]. They're drawing pools of blood and machetes and violent graphic things [. . .]. It was a lifeline, it was a safe way for them to dump that, to get it out there, to share it, to get it off their shoulders. And then at that point she was able to come alongside and look at the paper with them and connect. This fundamental shift, that's so simple,

but like is game-changing and life-changing, going from, you know, "tell me about the unspeakable" to coming alongside somebody and looking at their drawing. The page is holding your eye contact and it's way less direct and intimidating.

This was Romjue's "aha" moment. As a musician, he understood the power of music and although he didn't know the first thing about art therapy, he grasped the concept intuitively. The arts are vital for everyone, maybe especially trauma survivors.

He reached out to IJM's head of aftercare, who he had met when he went to the offices in DC. He asked if she had ever heard stories like the one his friend told him. Indeed, she had heard those stories and explained to Romjue that art therapy is a legitimate form of intervention. The problem, she went on to explain, was sustainability. Music and art therapists don't stay very long in the places they serve. They travel to Kenya, Cambodia, or Latin America to lead workshops, but then they leave. Local staff cannot sustain the services. Local aftercare providers are not trained as counselors or art therapists. He understood the explanation even if he didn't accept the logic.

> I was thinking about that—the vast majority of people that are caring for survivors of trauma who don't have letters behind their name. They haven't had access to formal education. They're community members that are serving in their own language and their own culture. They care deeply about the people, but they don't have mental health degrees. They don't have, even if, you know, the arts are accessible, they don't have music or art therapy degrees.

Romjue felt bothered by the lack of supportive infrastructure. He couldn't accept that there was a helpful solution out there, but no way of making it accessible and durable. "When words failed," said Romjue, "art and beauty were inviting and provided a lifeline for those kids to be able to unlock the door that was closed in their healing process, and their ability to connect." It was clear to him that trauma survivors need sustained access to the healing power of the arts. That meant that local lay care providers needed training in art therapy techniques.

Romjue smiled as he recalled the charm of his epistemic journey. He was a musician. He had no letters after his name. Yet he taught himself the meaning of words like aftercare and art therapy.

> I found myself in a place where I was naïve enough without a mental health degree to, you know, kind of start chewing on the toenail of

the elephant, like not really knowing what you're getting into, but it's, yeah, I can look back and you know, I've learned, I've gotten kind of a backseat degree in mental health where it's like I know the neurobiology of trauma now.

He earned his backseat degree by reaching out to experts. He created what he now calls an advisory council. He reached out to the head of music therapy at Seattle Children's Hospital, an art therapist he knew of at George Washington University, some dance and drama therapists. He also established a research partnership with the Seattle School of Theology and Psychology where sixty upper-level graduate students produced scores of literature reviews on art therapy.

Two years later, in 2012, he and a small team piloted a program in the Philippines. He called his burgeoning nonprofit, First Aid Arts. Their mission was to expand access to tried-and-true art therapy interventions by packaging them in such a way that they would be teachable and easily replicated by lay care providers. Hence, the name first aid, meant to convey layperson access to immediate and beneficial interventions within a relatively limited scope. During the pilot program, he and his team experienced a breakthrough with a teenage girl who had, for six months, been unresponsive to talk therapy. She was a trafficking survivor.

> This girl had access to this activity that's a piece of paper folded in half. On the front it says, "how others see me," and then you fold it up and it says, "how I see myself" and then "how I want to be seen" on the last page. And, for her, that was a lifeline that got her on the first rung of the ladder to begin stepping out of—unpacking—what she'd been through when she couldn't talk about it. She could respond to those prompts by coloring, by writing, by cutting out pictures.

Romjue likened the phenomenon to recent public interest in adult coloring books.[4] He described them as exercises in mindfulness. "It makes you here and now, and, breathing and pushing pigment around on a piece of paper that already looks beautiful. Because it's got an image in it that's black and white, that then mitigates the fear of creative risk," he said. By contrast, he explained how a blank piece of paper can be intimidating and how easy it is to be discouraged. Romjue gave an example of such debilitating mental self-talk, "I'm going to draw a crappy stick figure and I'll be embarrassed." This is why First Aid Arts uses attractive templates and questionnaires. They mitigate creative risk and invite participation.

According to Romjue, each of us comes fully stocked with creative potential, or "creative muscles" as he calls them. "We're all innovative, we're all creative, and these body-based experiences are good for us," he said. Especially for people from cultures where schooling disciplines students to become what Romjue calls "brains on a stick." Ironically, Romjue's parents were schoolteachers. They met in Hawaii teaching at a secondary school. His father taught English and Social Studies. His mother taught Physical Education. Romjue and his brother were born in Oahu and grew up bouncing between Hawaii and the Pacific Northwest for most of their young adult lives. They spent summers on a boat in Honolulu working, surfing, and visiting friends. Romjue loved his childhood. In many ways it kept his focus on life's simple pleasures—making new friends and exploring the natural world. Later, as a young adult he began to ponder career options and simply said to himself, "Whatever I do, if I can just make as much as a teacher, I'll live a very happy life." This, in spite of the fact that teachers in the US are notoriously underpaid, especially in comparison to their pay in other countries.[5] Alleviating the pressure of a grand career ambition opened possibilities for Romjue to pursue his heart's work.

AFTER THE PILOT PROGRAM in the Philippines, Romjue tweaked the curriculum and toolkit to run another pilot in Mexico City working with lay care providers who work in youth homes. He also made adjustments to offer programs back in Seattle once he got home. While working in Seattle, Romjue realized that First Aid Arts could expand to assist lay care providers in other domains as well. He began to offer local training for people in the US who were working with refugees, homeless, victims of torture, or members of school districts where school shootings had occurred.

Once again, he found himself in over his head, so he did what had worked before. He turned to experts for guidance. He established a few more advisory councils to help him identify demographic-specific interventions for particular sets of circumstances. For example, he created a Refugee Advisory Council with a curriculum designed to address the felt needs in that context. He brought on people like Dr. Nisha Sajnani who also works on the Harvard Project of Refugee Trauma. "I've just been blessed with some very gifted people that have been really generous with their expertise," said Romjue. He told me he was in the process of assembling an advisory council to focus on understanding needs in the context of natural disasters.

Year by year, First Aid Arts extended its reach to include curricula for all sorts of populations from aftercare givers in a refugee camp in Azraq,

Jordan, to individuals and groups in Kenya, Austria, and all over the United States. As of this writing, First Aid Arts has trained approximately 1,500 staff and volunteer caregivers from over 250 organizations in more than 56 countries. There's a poem by Rainer Maria Rilke about living life in ever widening circles that reach out across the world. "I may not complete this last one, but I give myself to it," he writes.[6] This sort of expansion describes Romjue's movement and perspective. He gives himself over to process in such a way that outcomes circle back to process.

In fact, he casually waived off the all-too-common nonprofit concern over mission drift with a smile by saying that his mission has always been "to help as many people as possible." In the last ten years, First Aid Arts has, in Romjue's words, "trained everybody from human trafficking aftercare providers in the Philippines, to a house mom in Ballard going through a divorce, to someone who had a cancer diagnosis, to someone who has a child that they're concerned about." While his target audience remains "the most in need and the least served" he has also been willing to expand his service outward to include those who he refers to as "just average people, your average Joe and Jane, not just you know, people who have gone through extreme trauma." Romjue's general policy of "helping as many people as possible" has paid off in ways he had not expected.

By opening his workshops to include stressed out Amazon employees, for example, he has been able to use their booking fee proceeds to offer scholarships to those who otherwise couldn't afford to attend. He has also found that some of his financially secure participants have become donors or sustaining members because of the positive experiences they've had at workshops. Currently First Aid Arts offers a host of programs including an introductory workshop, two levels of arts-based care workshops, and partner program training designed for specific populations. Most recently, Romjue added workplace workshops to help employees cope with toxic stress. First Aid Arts has offered training for individuals and organizations who want to use the arts to support survivors of natural disasters, human trafficking, forced migration, domestic violence, and homelessness for more than ten years now. According to the website, the nonprofit exists "for people just like you to create a world where wounded hearts heal beautifully."[7]

At the time of our interview, Romjue was getting ready to go to Jordan to work with people caring for Syrian refugees. I asked if he ever experienced compassion fatigue, or what psychologists sometimes call secondary traumatic stress characterized by emotional exhaustion from constant empathizing with people who are suffering. While he said there are times when he feels discouraged, he finds solace in the idea that he is not alone. "It's not going to pass or fail based on me. That's part of it," he said, "being able to rest and to see that I'm part of a bigger community." This perspective helps him push back on ideas his ego may give him about what he calls "that savior complex." In those moments he says to himself, "Chill out! Take comfort in your smallness." To elaborate on this point, he told a story about taking his nine-year-old daughter on a field trip to learn about the locks system in Lake Washington's ship canal. The tour guide gave a history of how the lock system came into being and how the project experienced an inordinate amount of red tape and gridlock. Then at some point, one man just started digging.

> Some dude just took a pic and went down and started, right by UW, just started dredging the canal by himself, like a shovelful at a time, and then other people joined around him and then it was one of those things where like, I believe in this, I'm going to do my part, I know that [. . .] I could spend my whole life and only complete a small portion of it, but it's just one of those things when there's, when there's something real going on and then you go for it [. . .] you kind of sound the horn to welcome other people to just like stop talking and start doing something.

He said his journey with First Aid Arts has felt a little bit like that experience. He heard the horn sound as a college student at Haugen's lecture on human trafficking and he has been shoveling away ever since. He has never felt alone in the process, though, and he uses moments of discouragement to refine his motivation. Whenever he feels like quitting, he plays devil's advocate with himself asking why he wants to quit and what he plans to do instead. He calls that a gift of the process because it helps him purify his motivation.

For Romjue, self-scrutiny tunes him into what he calls his "resonant frequencies." He used the metaphor of rubbing the rim of a wine glass to make it sing. "If you can pay attention to what your resonant frequencies are, like what makes your heart, if your heart is that wine glass, like what is it that will bring that little hum?" Romjue explained that when you find those things that make your heart come alive, you should work toward those things, and invest in those things. Likewise, when you find those things in your life that break your heart, that shatter your glass, you should move toward those things as well. It is a process of tuning in and opening up. "I call it a fertile question," explained Romjue. "What do you love? And what do you hate?" According to Romjue, if you can connect those two things, you're onto something.[8] I thought about our trip up the stairs to his office. He wanted to know my story, what I was about, what interested me, what bothered me. Although I was distracted at the time, I can see now that he was curious about my resonant frequencies. What did I love? What did I want? Fertile questions, indeed.

Reflection

Romjue's story highlights the value of adopting curiosity as a default mode. Scholars often conceptualize curiosity as an epistemic virtue—a love of learning that serves knowledge acquisition. But through Romjue's story, we glimpse the social function of curiosity. His curiosity is directed inward as much as it is outward. For Romjue, curiosity relies on attentiveness and openness. It implies taking an interest. At the same time, it goes beyond (mere) attentiveness by contemplating observations and asking questions. There is a forward momentum to curiosity that is lacking in attentiveness. Attentiveness without curiosity cannot be sustained.

Curiosity takes a person further because they learn things they otherwise would not. Curiosity involves what philosopher Elias Baumgarten calls "a questioning spirit," animated by choice and judgment.[9] A person selects some things over others and judges that they are worth learning about. Etymologically, curiosity is linked to care and concern through its Latin root, curare, which means to take care of. In this way, curiosity, long considered an epistemic virtue, could also be considered a moral virtue related to receptivity and reverence.

Curiosity serves phronesis because it is an open and receptive quality of attention that propels someone to deepen their understanding of and sensitivity to the pressures affecting the context of concern. We can see the circular movement of Romjue's curiosity through this story. He begins with himself (inward curiosity) as a young college student after hearing a lecture about slavery and human trafficking on his campus. He asks himself, "How can I help? I don't have money to give . . . what does it look like for me to show up?'" At first, he works within the bounds of his ability and knowledgebase, playing music to raise money and spread awareness.

All the while, curiosity pushes him to continue learning about the particulars of the context of concern, expanding the bounds of his knowledge base. Eventually, he witnesses first-hand the limitations of the mode of justice he has been supporting through his music and wonders about alternatives, "If you really want sustainable emancipation, you can't just knock a door down and grab someone from the situation." His critical reflection leads him to a more nuanced understanding of the limits of aftercare, "I was thinking about that—the vast majority of people that are caring for survivors of trauma who don't have letters behind their name." Then his curiosity circles back to himself once again, wondering how he, specifically, could contribute.

Romjue makes use of his positionality and skill set to assemble a team of experts who could brainstorm with him along with each other ways to make aftercare more sustainable and art therapy more accessible among communities struggling to support victims of human trafficking. Like Lent from Dance Peace, Romjue underscores the value of building partnerships and establishing community. Both Lent and Romjue value and trust their partners implicitly. More than that, the collaboration allows them to dilate the self, so to speak and, as Romjue puts it, "take comfort in [their] smallness" by recognizing that success or failure does not depend on a single person, that outcomes are beyond the control of the personal ego.

Notably, Romjue demonstrates how his smallness and lack of control does not impede his impulse to act. He refers to the story of the Ballard Locks system and how "some dude just started dredging the canal by himself, like a shovel full at a time." His recounting of that story reminds me of an image Martin Luther King Jr. used in his famous "I Have a Dream" speech. King asks his audience "to hew out of the mountain of despair a stone of hope."[10] One stone, like one shovel full, is all we need to do. As Romjue acknowledges, "I could spend my whole life and only complete a small portion." His sentiment, again, echoing King's "I may not get there with you" from his final "Mountaintop Speech."[11] Romjue, like King, exhibits faith. His openness, curiosity, and heart-first approach reflect an almost childlike expectation for goodness, all despite having seen how painful the world can be.

The next chapter introduces someone whose activism reflects a similar sort of faith, even though he self-identifies as "not a religious person." Gidon Bromberg is a lawyer and activist who, up until the official war broke out in 2023, was working to protect the already war-torn Gaza Strip and Jordan River Basin from further environmental degradation. As a lawyer he grounds his arguments in reason and logic, but the chaos and contingency of his immediate context requires a certain level of surrender.

THREE

See from the Outside

Streams are very visual—they very much speak
to the necessity to work together because
literally they don't respect the borders.

—GIDON BROMBERG

Even though I read his professional biography online and knew he grew up in Australia, Gidon Bromberg's Aussie accent caught me by surprise. He had been living in Israel for nearly thirty years leading a regional environmental initiative called EcoPeace that brings people together from Jordan, Palestine, and Israel to advocate on behalf of the environment. He has become a central figure in sustainability efforts and peace advancement in the Middle East.

I was speaking to him from his office in Tel Aviv. At the time of our interview (late 2019), a series of weekly protests had been occurring for more than six months at the Gaza border. The mass resistance protests, called the Great March of Return, demanded a Palestinian right to return to the lands from which they were displaced in 1948.[1] Protestors also objected to Israel's blockade of Gaza and the US's recent recognition of Jerusalem as capital of Israel.[2] "There's so much blood lost over the land [we] claim to love," said Bromberg. "[We] claim to love it, but we're polluting this land. We're poisoning this land at horrific rates." Bromberg speaks with an unwavering conviction. The environmental reality he describes is deadly serious—97 percent of Gaza's groundwater is not suitable for human consumption—yet there's a lilt, a playfulness to his voice. He often smiled, incredulously, at the enormity of human oversight. I don't know what I would call that something I could hear in his voice. It wasn't quite optimism, or even hope. It sounded, to me, like faith.

For Bromberg, environmental stewardship is a moral imperative, and for him personally, a calling. He spoke about his work as if it were a vocation, not a job. I'm not sure he would like me to describe him as having faith since he self-identifies as nonreligious, but the type of faith I'm talking about has little to do with piety or religion. It's a gritty kind of faith that comes more from discipline than it does devotion. This type of faith is a perspective, which accepts with confidence the present moment, even in its ugliness and sorrow. Bromberg has been around too long for naïve optimism or wishful thinking. For three decades he has been working on cross-border water issues in the context of the world's most enduring conflict. He has watched peace ebb and flow in the region for half his life.

BROMBERG FELT CALLED to Israel at a young age. He was born there but his parents left for Australia when he was just three years old. He returned for the first time as an eleven-year-old in 1970 to attend his grandfather's funeral. The only reason his mother brought him along was because he was a cheap travel companion. "At that time, if you were under twelve, you were half a ticket," he smiled. During that trip Bromberg learned he had 30 first cousins. "It was a wonderful experience, to suddenly experience family, to have fun in a completely different environment . . . They're all playing football in the street, while in Australia, I'm watching television," he recalled. The trip so influenced Bromberg that, on the plane ride home, he told his mother that he would live in Israel when he grew up. Bromberg kept his promise by not only living in Israel, but by becoming one of the biggest advocates for the health of its ecosystem.[3] The eventuality of his return, however, took decades in the making.

Growing up back in Australia, he was certain he would return to Israel someday, but he was not sure what his role would be once he got there. After college he attended law school with the vague idea that he could use a law degree to address human rights issues in Israel. As a law student at Monash University in Australia, he began to refine his interests in the law by recognizing climate issues as human rights issues. In the 1980s, along with thousands of protestors, many of whom were university students like him, Bromberg rallied to block the construction of a dam that would destroy Australia's last wild river, the Franklin. He was particularly interested in the legal aspects of the case. The federal government designated the proposed construction site a world heritage site, but the state government sought development and wanted a dam to produce hydroelectricity. A legal battle between the federal government and the Tasmanian government ensued which resulted in a landmark High Court ruling in the federal government's favor. The environmentalists won. Bromberg was exhilarated, "It was my first experience with bottom-up advocacy combined with top-down policy," a combination that would eventually be the basis for EcoPeace. Two weeks after graduation, he boarded a plane for Israel. He didn't even sit for the bar in Australia.

Upon returning to his beloved country with his new focus on environmental law, Bromberg could more clearly see how decades of conflict were impacting the environment. Whether short-lived or decades-long, conflict disrupts positive human practices needed for sustainable living. Irrigation systems go unmanaged, trees go unplanted, agricultural terraces are not seasonally rebuilt. As people are forced into mobility and migration, they cannot form communities or make long-term investments in the land. So, not only are there direct costs (i.e., resource grabs, human displacement, and toxins introduced by various weapons and artillery), but there are innumerable indirect consequences as well.

Conflict forces people to make poor decisions based on short-term time horizons. Professor Ken Conca, who teaches environmental peacebuilding courses at American University, gives the example of the Nagorno–Karabakh conflict, where people cut down their own fruit and nut orchards for timber because staying on the land for the next harvest season was not a reliable option.[4] Conflict turns a singular ecosystem into fragmented and bordered territories. It causes people to make abnormally rash decisions like overfishing or turning forests into charcoal.

One of the most gut-wrenching sights for Bromberg when he returned to Israel in the 1990s was the state of the River Jordan, a once-powerful holy river that pumped turbines to provide electricity. It was now so over-extracted and choked with sewage that it could barely turn a mouse wheel. Meanwhile, neighboring Jordan's population expanded to include refugees who fled violence in Iraq and Syria. And they did not have drinkable water. Although the environmental reality was worsening, Bromberg felt encouraged by the burgeoning promise of political peace. The Israeli government's Prime Minister, Yitzhak Rabin, and the leader of the Palestine Liberation Organization (PLO), Yasser Arafat, had recently signed the Oslo Declaration to plot Palestinian self-government and formally end the First Intifada.[5] "The mood was euphoric," recalled Bromberg. We all expected within five years there would be two states—a Palestinian state next to the state of Israel. We were all certain about that, and there was consensus among us that that's the vision that we wanted."

In 1994 peace seemed like an inevitability, so Bromberg enrolled in a graduate program at American University to study the environmental implications of peace in the Middle East. His research surveyed and analyzed some of the proposed peace projects. What he found was that enthusiasm for peace centered on commercial progress rather than environmental protection. "There was very little environmental and carrying capacity thinking in the peace negotiations," explained Bromberg. He went on:

> An example is that, you know, there were 50,000 new hotel rooms being proposed around the Dead Sea by the Israeli side, by the Jordanian side, by the Palestinian side—without anyone thinking through the accumulated impact of building so many hotels. Where would the water come from, how would the sewage be treated? Think of all the additional infrastructure that would need to be built and how that would impact this rather small lake. The Dead Sea is actually just a small lake.[6]

The plans also included an eight-lane superhighway cutting through the Jordan Rift Valley to connect Cairo to Istanbul and move goods between Africa, Europe, and Asia. The thinking was that the peace process would include peace with Syria, Jordan, Iraq, and Iran, so Road 19 Israel, which ends at the border between Israel and Lebanon, could continue from Lebanon through Syria then into Turkey and into mainland Europe. Peace, it turned out, did not look so good for the environment.[7]

In order to modify the peace agenda to include care for the environment, Bromberg knew he needed backup. His voice would be stronger in a chorus. "But as far as getting people around the table, you know, in '94 when this research was done, there's no internet. There's no Google." He chuckled at the memory—spending hours at the library pouring over books, trying to identify environmental leaders in the Arab world. He found a book that included an inventory of Middle Eastern Environmental NGOs. "I contacted them through the use of *fax*! You know what a fax is?" he laughed. He also wrote letters, which he emphasized were typed on a typewriter. The letters were invitations to a meeting. When he received no response, he followed up with phone calls. It took effort to convince potential Arab partners that, although it was risky, it was worthwhile to at least meet with him to see what could be done.

Bromberg had never sat down with a Palestinian colleague to talk about the environment before. "That wasn't thinkable before the signing of the Oslo Accords . . . it was actually illegal." He continued, "Although I had a fear, it was a combination of fear and excitement for—for the unknown nature of it, of the potential of what we can do together." Before he left Washington, DC with a degree in International Environmental Law, he raised

$20,000 to start a regional NGO. "That gave enough money just to bring 16 people together." His goal was to convince four Egyptians, four Palestinians, four Jordanians, and four Israelis, each from different organizations to meet in the town of Taba, Egypt. To achieve that, however, he had to gain their trust by meeting with each of them individually. "I certainly remember the butterflies in my stomach . . . I'm there, you know, 'is this dangerous what I'm doing?'" He had never driven "beyond the old city," as he called it.

As he drove, his mind raced. He tried to calm himself with the reminder that he personally chose this person after researching his credentials and studying the work he had done. He understood who he was professionally and had a sense for what he cared about and what they could do together. But he still couldn't shake the fear. "I didn't know their personal story," he explained, "maybe someone close in their family was killed. I didn't know the level of hate, if there was hate. I think I didn't feel it—any hate, because I didn't grow up in the conflict. I grew up outside the conflict." Bromberg's outsider status gave him the audacity to challenge the status quo and identify opportunities that insiders could not see.

BROMBERG SELECTED the town of Taba for the initial meeting because his research told him that Egypt was leading the world in environmental issues. He wanted his collaborators to feel at home. "You've got to be sensitive to the existing politics," he said. As sensitive as he was, he still had a difficult time convincing his partners in Jordan. As Bromberg explained, "Jordanians didn't know Israelis at all. And that was very difficult. Only one Jordanian agreed to come to that first meeting in Taba." Palestinians, however, were more comfortable with the arrangement. Many Israelis knew Palestinians and vice versa. Their century-long feud inspired a sort of intimacy. Bromberg put it simply, "We share the same piece of Earth," he said.

The simple truth, for all parties involved, is that they can't disengage from one another, especially when it comes to water issues. "If our neighbor fails in water sanitation then that failure won't just stop on their side. It'll cross over." He went on to cite Gaza as an example. "Gaza is collapsing with sewage, but that sewage is not just polluting the waters of Gaza and the beaches of Gaza, it's being carried by the currents to the beaches of Israel." Bromberg saw an opportunity to refine his project once again to focus on water.

Streams are very visual—they very much speak to the necessity to work together because literally they don't respect the borders and you can follow the stream to the—to the green line and look at [. . .] your reality, your neighbor's reality right in front of you. It's in your face. That's the real strength of water issues—they flow, they cross borders. They're a fantastically strong example of common concern.

Even with such a convincing metaphor for the region's interdependence, Bromberg struggled to get meaningful buy-in from his colleagues at the meeting. They agreed that the environmental community should have a voice in the peace process, but they weren't quite ready to commit themselves to a regional NGO. As Bromberg put it, "Although we were all euphoric about peace, still, you know, there was a lack of trust and concern that things wouldn't work out in some way."

Working with the other is risky. By focusing on water, Bromberg argued that they could defend themselves against condemnation. Water, after all, is the essence of human life. He remembered giving a motivational speech at the meeting in which he said something like, "We are not traitors; we are actually the most loyal people to our communities because we are looking after their interests." Still, he had to acknowledge what he was up against, "There are groups, individuals, organizations, societies that simply see the other as the enemy and if you were working with the other you must be working for the enemy. That's their paradigm. That's their outlook on life." But advocating on behalf of water access offered a clear line of defense. Bromberg continued reenacting his motivational speech:

> When someone condemns you for working with the other side on water issues, you're empowered to respond. "What exactly do you want me to do? We can't live without water; we can't survive without water. Don't tell me that I'm working for the other, I'm working for myself and my community."

By the end of the three-day meeting, Bromberg received tentative support. He took what he could get. That was enough for him to begin building EcoPeace Middle East. He brought on two codirectors—Munqeth Mehyar from Jordan and Nader Al-Khateeb from Palestine. They sought to capitalize on the momentum established by the Oslo Accords, seeing it as "a window of opportunity" to get environmental protection included in the peace process.

Yet defending themselves against condemnation became a distracting side-project for the leaders of EcoPeace. Not only were they perceived to be working with the other, but they were also perceived as delaying the peace process. There were several exciting development projects on the horizon and Bromberg and his do-gooder environmentalists were seen as delaying "the benefits of peace." Developers created a false dichotomy between peace and sustainability by labeling projects like the proposed superhighway the "peace highway." Those labels, Bromberg explained, "made it very difficult for the environmental community to come and say, 'yeah, but let's reconsider this project for the environmental concerns.'" Within a few years the proposed peace projects, environmentally sound or not, became moot. Negotiations at Camp David failed, bus bombings and suicide attacks resumed with renewed vigor, eventually giving way to the Second Intifada.

EcoPeace offices started to receive what Bromberg described as "ugly correspondence." Staff members became ostracized for continuing to work with the other. Family members cut ties. The Jordanian director was shot at. Then in 1998, EcoPeace was forced to close its office in Cairo. "The Mubarak regime ordered that our office in Cairo be closed because they didn't like the fact that Egyptian Greenies were talking to Israeli Greenies. They saw that as a threat to Egyptian national security," Bromberg explained.

IN THE MIDST OF INCREASING VIOLENCE, the EcoPeace codirectors decided to narrow their focus to addressing the immediate concerns of people in their respective communities. Bromberg recalled the satisfaction he felt back in college doing local activism in opposition to the dam construction. It was time for him to return to his grassroots.

After four years of top-down advocacy efforts, EcoPeace shifted its emphasis to bottom-up, community-led activism. They did beach cleanups and educational initiatives on the coral reefs. The goal was to work very locally on shared water bodies to build trust, cooperation, and improve the reality on the ground. It was the beginning of what would later be recognized as environmental peacebuilding.

> We did a beautiful event of the release of turtles that were being bred. And we did this with Jordanian and Israeli youth, kids. Just you know, on boats in the middle of the ocean there on the border, releasing baby turtles together. We had some beautiful moments, stunning, but I mean this was particularly beautiful. This is particularly emotional. The excitement of kids releasing turtles into the shared ocean, the Red Sea, the Gulf of Aqaba.

Working with children inspired Bromberg to initiate the Good Water Neighbors program in 2001. "Kids immediately understand," he said, "They get it that they need to know what their neighbors are doing, that they can never clean up their river if their neighbor doesn't clean up the river too." Bromberg saw something of himself in the children he worked with. "Young people are born with a level of optimism, with a level of innocence that is really empowering, that reminds you not to give up. There's no possibility to even think about giving up. This is too important. This is their future. It's our future."

One of the projects carried out by Good Water Neighbors was developing a walking path connecting an Israeli community with a Palestinian community. Bromberg called it "the neighbors path trail" and explained that it "enables the community to literally see each other beyond the fence." He said the trail system was effective because it brought people out of their communities and to the border.

> The border area has been an area that you stay away from, you don't go to the border. The border is where the enemy is, and the border is where there is a greater risk of violence [. . .]. People didn't go to the border because they would just see offense. They didn't know what they were looking for. The good neighbors' trails asked them to look at the water.

Educational signage along the walking path explains water sources, points out cross-border basins, highlights sites of cultural heritage, and heavily emphasizes the demise of the Jordan River. "We'd show photos of how the river used to look and people were shocked. 'How could this be? How could we have turned the River Jordan or any other rivers into sewage canals?'" The trail project introduces new concepts to community members and helps to trouble existing enemy relationships. Once he saw how influential it was, Bromberg sought to expand on Good Water Neighbors.

He launched a pilot program that began with five communities, four of the pairs being Israeli–Palestinian and one pair being Israeli–Jordanian, and a staff person on each side working to advance cooperative work across the border. The project was going well with funding from the European Union (EU) until the Second Intifada, when Bromberg received a letter saying, "the circumstances will no longer allow you to implement this project." The EU cut his funding.

In a panic, Bromberg and his codirectors flew to Brussels with the hope of changing their decision. "We literally knocked on the door of the relevant commissioner and insisted we meet." He grinned at the memory. "Giving up was not on the agenda," adding, "That's just never been on the agenda." In the end, they were able to convince the EU commissioner that the Second Intifada made the project *more* important, not less. Bromberg said his argument went something like, "You're saying there's no hope in the region. We're saying no, we will create that hope, it's not going to happen by itself. This is exactly the role that you should be playing, you shouldn't be walking out. You should be coming in, stronger than ever!" He smiled victoriously then added:

> We actually convinced the commissioner not to cancel the project [. . .] now, I can tell you we've lost out on projects [laughs] but that one was saved because we were so determined. "You tell us that we're hopeless? We know the situation's difficult but don't turn us into a hopeless region. We refuse to accept that. There's hope in our region and we're going to create that hope."

Just like the environmentalist victory against the Franklin River dam construction in Australia, Bromberg once again felt exhilarated and empowered. "Having survived the Second Intifada," he said, "I guess our stance is that nothing will ever stop us, nothing can close this down now." He went on to describe some of his favorite Good Water Neighbors projects.

In 2007 he organized an event called The Big Jump, where three mayors, one from Israel, one from Palestine, and one from Jordan jumped into the Jordan River together. The event took years to materialize and all of Bromberg's powers of persuasion. Ultimately the jump happened, not out of friendship, but out of mutual recognition for their shared destiny. "If they're to achieve the type of prosperity and benefits that they desire for their community," said Bromberg, "they literally needed to get wet together." As a telling sidenote, the mayors had to jump into a tributary because the Jordan River is too polluted.

EcoPeace also recently hosted a regional teachers' meeting where 50 teachers, one-third Palestinian, one-third Jordanian, and one-third Israeli, came and spent four days together talking about climate change and regional environmental concerns and how they planned to address those issues in their respective classrooms.

> It doesn't mean that these teachers have become best friends. It doesn't mean that these kids or these mayors are no longer part of the region, are somehow dreamers out of context. They're not. They're going to be condemned and they need to be really careful, but they are so empowered, they are so enriched by the information they received and the seed of hope that has been planted in their hearts. You can feel it, you can see

it. That is a miracle. In the end, I'm not a religious person and for me, it speaks to the humanity in our souls that despite the suffering that all sides experienced in these last hundred years, despite that, there is this essence of humanity that has just been waiting to come out.

Just before our interview in 2019, Bromberg and the other EcoPeace directors accepted an invitation to speak at the UN Security Council for the US Surgeon General's Climate Summit.[8] They had also just recently spoken with the Vatican at the Munich Security Conference. Their message that water security is a national security issue is gaining attention on the international stage because it productively reinterprets an existing paradigm. EcoPeace uses the state of the environment to broaden conventional conceptions of security from military security to human and climate security.

Broadening the definition of security opens up new possibilities for negotiation and compromise. Previously, peace talks in the Middle East operated as a zero-sum game. Bromberg lamented:

It's no wonder that the vast majority of the public in Israel and in Palestine have no belief that peace is ever going to be happening, is ever going to break out, because in the last 25 years we haven't been able to agree on everything and, therefore, if we haven't agreed on everything, we haven't been able to move forward on anything. We can change that and we need to learn from the failure of the approach.

As I write this, tensions between Israel and Palestine are on the rise, making any steps toward peace seem like a daydream. The region is experiencing an escalation of violence reminiscent of the last two intifadas. Analysts attribute the spike in volatility to Israel's new extreme-right coalition government led by Prime Minister Benjamin Netanyahu.[9]

Still, Bromberg refuses to give up. At the recent UN Security Council meeting, he made a case for new water technology development in the region, asking the Council to urge Israelis, Palestinians, and Jordanians to work together toward its advancement. He likened the cooperation to the coal and steel agreements made between the US and Europe after World War II. He said working together on water could similarly lay the groundwork for sustainable peace. "Good water, and not necessarily good fences, make good neighbors," said Bromberg. Adding, "Let us set water free to give life and hope to our region."[10] To me, he talked about how his focus on water participates in dismantling the existing zero-sum paradigm. He said:

It's not that we don't want to see everything resolved tomorrow, we do, but if we can't resolve everything tomorrow, but we can resolve one of the issues tomorrow and that helps improve the reality on the ground, if that helps build trust, if that helps show that there is a path there on a critical issue like water, then why isn't there a path there, why wouldn't there be a path there for the other critical issues?

Toward the end of our interview, Bromberg described his vision for new water technology and his goal for EcoPeace. He wants Jordan to become a major producer of renewable energy by harnessing solar power and selling their electricity to Israel and Palestine. Jordan's vast desert offers a comparable advantage when it comes to solar energy. And Israel and Palestine, on the Mediterranean, can use that renewable energy to desalinate marine water and sell it back. "Solar power moving west, opens the door for water to move east," Bromberg explained, "That's a big, powerful, game-changing project on the horizon." His eyebrows raised as he smiled. He knows it's his most ambitious project, yet. I smiled too, realizing that all his efforts abide in a sort of natural order, whether it is water's irreverence for territories, or the movement of the sun from East to West.

Reflection

In the opening chapter I considered the value of strangerhood and how, even in our otherness, we must "establish an ethics of reciprocal responsibility." I described two types of strangers—one who comes in to resolve local disputes and another who seeks inclusion and adopts local norms. Each of these, I argued, have their own limitations in terms of civic engagement, but an amalgam of the two potentiates phronesis. Bromberg exhibits qualities of both.

Like the first type of stranger, he is an expert and an outsider. He grew up in Australia, so his perspective allowed him to see possibilities for collaboration that were foreclosed to locals. As an environmental expert, Bromberg drew attention to the water crisis, framing it as a dilemma. Sometimes dilemmas create a scenario in which groups, normally unwilling to come together or stand apart from conflict, are forced into making evaluations and judgments.

Still, like the second type of stranger, he understood and had respect for the precarity of the local order. He might be new to the conflict, but he is now a permanent resident. Bromberg's positionality allowed him to see the dualities for what they are and allowed him to occupy a space betwixt and between ("Although I had a fear, it was a combination of fear and excitement for—for the unknown nature of it, of the potential of what we can do together").[11]

In some ways, Bromberg's role as insider–outsider reminds me of the mythic trickster figure. Broadly speaking, Trickster is a figure of hope and futurity because the trickster spirit is utopian.[12] As Kamala Visweswaran writes, trickster's modus operandi is manifestly to "faire semblant," to act "as if" things are not as they are, or that utopia is already in progress.[13] Acting "as if" enables an audacity that allows Trickster to take necessary, even if unusual or outlandish, steps toward (re)making the world.[14] A benefit of embracing our mutual strangerhood is that it opens the door for a trickster spirit to shake loose some of the calcified conventions that inhibit growth and expansion. Bromberg arrived on the scene following the Oslo Accords when peace seemed imminent. He described the mood as "euphoric" and said he used Oslo as "a window of opportunity" to get environmental protection included in the peace process (kairos). Thirty years, and two intifadas later, Bromberg spoke in our interview "as if" peace was already in progress. As I prepared this manuscript for the final stages of production, a formal war broke out between Israel and Hamas. I sent an e-mail to Bromberg to check on his safety and express my condolences. He said he had no words to convey the tragedy of the situation and ended his message with the line, "May we know better days."

Acting "as if" does not mean ignoring reality. It means engaging the moral imagination to see creative possibility. In his work with the Good Neighbors project, Bromberg acknowledges the very real constraints of the situation, "It doesn't mean that these teachers have become best friends. It doesn't mean that these kids or these mayors are no longer part of the region, are somehow dreamers out of context." Instead, he says the goal is to create a sustainable ethic of reciprocal responsibility, "Despite the suffering that all sides experienced in these last hundred years, despite that—there is this essence of humanity that has just been waiting to come out." Bromberg's story communicates the value of adopting the bifocal lens of the stranger. It allows him to tack back-and-forth between an aerial bird's eye view and a ground-level community activist view. A nimble perspective allows a person to envision both universal and local values, aiding in the phronetic capacity to preserve noble values, in unusual or complicated situations.

Both this chapter and the next refer to children as inspiration. Bromberg says he takes heart in the fact that "kids immediately understand" because they are uniquely positioned to see bi-focally—they are born into the conflict and learn to rationalize it using local values, attitudes, and beliefs, yet they maintain a certain fidelity to universal principles of love, justice, and compassion that allows them to grasp the moral significance and immediate importance of Bromberg's work. The next chapter introduces Estelle Brown who, like Bromberg, takes steps to create hope where it otherwise might not exist in her community. She, too, exhibits the beneficial qualities of strangerhood. She calls into question the normative order of things and pokes holes in existing structures and paradigms. Like Lent and Romjue (chapters 1 and 2), Brown keeps her mission relatively simple and her approach radically inclusive. Her story highlights the role of emotions like anger in fighting akrasia and how playful disobedience can be a form of phronesis.

FOUR

Embrace Maladjustment

It wasn't about growing food.
It was about starting a conversation.

— ESTELLE BROWN

In 2019, Estelle Brown and I sat together on a plump velour couch in the parlor of an old, recently restored bed and breakfast. The new owners moved to Todmorden, in Yorkshire, England, from South Africa a few years before because of the town's reputation for kindness, ingenuity, and youthful start-ups. The innkeeper, Jacob, a man in his early forties bustled about as Brown and I got settled. At breakfast, before Brown had arrived, Jacob told me he was excited to host Brown for our interview because she was the unofficial mayor of Todmorden. His enthusiasm made me nervous; I felt the Full English Breakfast I had just eaten do a somersault. As it turned out, Brown could not have been warmer. She smiles easily, uses self-deprecating humor, and has a mischievousness about her that belies her seventy-five years.

After introducing myself as a professor and while checking the levels on Brown's lapel mic, she told me about her college-age years growing up in the social, political heat of the 1960s. She expressed disappointment in today's youth, lamenting the fact that they are not proportionally outraged. She asked why universities weren't more engaged and actively provoking youthful passion. "Where are the campus protests and marches? Where are they?" she demanded. It was a rhetorical question, of course, and I agreed with her sentiment. Yet, I also felt responsible; Had I become part of the establishment? My breakfast did another somersault, and I sank deeper into the couch. "The spark's gone out," she said finally, "It's only us old ladies left with the spark." Her comment referred to her co-conspirator, a woman in her mid-sixties, Mary Clear, with whom she started the (now world famous) urban gardening project Incredible Edible Todmorden.

Brown began right away by telling me "How it all started." She said that in 2008 she and Mary got together "to have a moan." They talked about the lack of bugs on car windshields and the general recession of other species. They raised eyebrows over seed monopolies and the fact that "Monsanto sells corn that people can't collect seed from." They complained about greedy bankers and lazy governments. Mostly, they were angry. "The scientists know how to do it," Brown said exasperated.

> They can make a golf course in the middle of the desert in Sudan for rich people to knock balls around—they can grow in a desert, but they won't grow in Sudan to feed poor people because there's no money in that. It's all about money. It's all about the dollar and the Euro and—sorry—I'm getting angry now.

I told Brown she didn't need to apologize. In many ways, anger is the most appropriate response. And for her, anger always led to action. She has never been one to play victim. Besides, even when she's angry, her sparkling eyes look like they want to smile. She continued:

> So, what can we do? Well, we can reach the bits of land we've got in front of us, take them, don't ask permission, just take them, and grow food on them. So that's basically what we did. Because it wasn't about growing food. It was about starting a conversation.

The conversation Brown wanted to start goes beyond food, banking, supply chains, and the environment. In her mind, growing food to eat and share was a way for people to relearn kindness. Her rationale was simple. All the major religious and ethnic groups she could think of "celebrate by sharing food," she explained. "So, if we grew food that people could share, we could reach everybody. And it worked. It just worked," she said incredulously. Before they got started "guerilla gardening," she remembers Clear saying, "Well, we're okay because the prisons are full. They can't lock us up." Brown laughed. "So, that was it. We just went out. Policemen can lock me up. Please lock me up! Can you imagine the story? White-haired old lady put in prison for planting a carrot."

Brown and Clear along with some others began planting vegetables, herbs, and fruit trees in small bits of vacant land around town. They turned parking strips, unused lots, and bus stops into gardens. They called their initiative Incredible Edible Todmorden and told curious townspeople, "If you eat, you're in." Eventually the idea took hold, attracting volunteers and businesses to contribute public plots and elbow grease. Neighboring towns heard about "Oddmorden," as Brown calls it with affection, bringing regional tourism to the small town. As tourism expanded, Incredible Edible Todmorden received worldwide publicity and media attention. Sociologists and agricultural scholars from around the world have come to Todmorden to study their open-source produce model and at least fifteen other towns in the UK have created their own version of Incredible Edible.[1]

It would be unfair to characterize Incredible Edible Todmorden as an overnight success, however. And not all of the townspeople were immediately fond of the idea. Brown told me a story about how she ended up illegally spreading wildflower seeds all over a privately-owned lot in Todmorden because the landowner refused her request to turn the lot into a wildflower meadow. The land had been home to an old mill, one of the last in the little West Yorkshire town. When the mill was demolished, Brown began collecting buckets of native wildflower seeds donated by local shops with the idea of returning the space to a meadow again. The landowner's refusal stood in the way of her dream.

> So, we took the seeds out, put them into bags, put the buckets [over] our heads, and then threw them all over the land and took photographs with pink buckets on our heads. You can tell who we all are, even with buckets on our heads. We did it anyways, nobody ever said a word. [pause, smiling] And it's still there, still growing wildflowers.

Brown is a self-described "old hippie" who loves to make trouble. As a young woman, she laid in front of buses during Europe's campaign for nuclear disarmament (the symbol for which became the universal peace sign in 1958). As a teenager, she "did the whole psychedelic thing" and paraded in London against the Vietnam War chanting her discontent with the then-US President, Lyndon Johnson ("Hey, hey LBJ, how many kids did you kill today?").[2] She was, and still is, adamant about peace. But she regrets being part of what she calls "the throwaway society"—a generation that gave little thought to the future.

> We thought we would die [. . .] we thought we'd got maybe a few years because of America and Russia and the Bay of Pigs and the nuclear submarines. We had already worked out where all the American air bases were. Because they wouldn't have bombed America because all the missile bases were in the UK, and they could reach the UK. They

couldn't reach America. So, we would have died, not Americans. So, we had worked out where the nearest air base was and if the four-minute warning went, we got as close to it as we could because we wanted to go up in a [makes a puff sound] rather than die of radiation sickness. It was all worked out. I was never going to be old. I'm not sure how I got to be this person.

Somewhat suddenly she found herself in her seventies looking back on a lifetime of "throwaway knickers, throwaway pens, throwaway razors, throwaway everything, because the world was going to go up in a big puff of smoke." When the world didn't combust, Brown looked around and noticed that after an evening drive her windshield was no longer "spattered with insects." She thought about all the creatures that have gone extinct in her lifetime and grew increasingly disturbed by their absence.

In the early 2000s, toward the end of her sixth decade, Brown and her husband moved to Todmorden, a small and struggling West Yorkshire town. In the mid-nineteenth century, Todmorden had bustled. The Industrial Revolution brought better roads, a railway station, and a canal passing through the town's center.[3] "It was one of the richest towns in the UK," said Brown. "The north was a lot richer than the south back then because all the industry was here, all the weaving mills were here, the Industrial Revolution happened here." Brown explained that there was a young and active workforce in Todmorden until around the 1960s "and then gradually after the 60s everything closed down. But the young people stayed because it's where their homes are, but now they were poor young people," she said. Todmorden is still relatively young with seven primary schools to serve all the children from the young families. It is also still relatively poor with an estimated 28 percent of the town's children living in poverty.[4] "We are a deprived area," Brown said, "Which should mean they throw money at us, but they don't. They just give us a label." Then she added with a bemused smile, "We don't think we're deprived. We think everything we've got around us is wonderful—the countryside, the hills." Brown looked out the window at the moorlands.

Brown's perspective, whether from pride or dogged optimism, her ability to see abundance and plentitude is ultimately what drew her to Todmorden and what led her to act on its behalf. It is not that she was in denial. Rather, she knew the town wasn't living up to its potential. "It was a dirty, filthy, depressing town with all the shops closed, hardly any cafes . . . [it] was in a bad way . . . massive vandalism, antisocial behavior, smashed shop windows, empty shops." She saw gardening as a practical solution to structural problems.

IRONICALLY, Todmorden is not the best place to plant fruits and vegetables. "It's glacial," Brown explained, "It's gritstone rock." She pointed to the hills outside the window. "All we can grow up there is horses and sheep. But the graveyard is good," she added. I couldn't help but laugh at her deadpan delivery. "We grow pumpkins in there. The after-school gardening club—there's a school next to the graveyard—they grow in there, between the gravestones." According to Brown, nowhere is off limits. The police station grows corn, the fire station has tomatoes, there are fruit trees seemingly everywhere.

Planted with each garden is a sign encouraging passersby to take whatever they wanted. But the idea of a community garden didn't catch on right away. "It took us nearly 18 months before people would take anything because it's terribly English not to take anything that isn't yours," she said. I suppressed a joke about colonization that Brown probably would have laughed at because I didn't want to interrupt her point about norms of English society. I'm an American, besides. Who am I to make that joke? But, to Brown's point, teaching people to take vegetables from a garden they didn't sow was a challenge, even now, it still is.

During my visit in 2019 I watched a woman sheepishly pluck some basil in a raised bed outside the police station. She noticed me watching her and said, "It says I'm supposed to take it." I emphatically reassured her that she was correct, but found it noteworthy that, even after ten years, the concept still feels strange to people. Brown said that's because it is harder to grow kindness than it is to grow food:

> One thing I've always said is any town can grow food, because it's in food's nature and a plant's nature to grow if you stick it in the ground, that's what it wants to do. So, any town could grow masses and masses of food. But if you haven't grown kindness and community with it, when trouble comes everyone's going to fight over that food. But if you grow caring and kindness and community along with the food, when trouble comes everyone will see everybody else has something. And they kind of go hand in hand. It's a natural progression.

It might be in "a plant's nature to grow," but that wasn't the experience Brown had at first. I assumed the idea for Incredible Edible came from a personal love for gardening. I was wrong. She corrected me. "No! All I grew was my fingernails," she exclaimed. "Very few of us knew how to grow anything. We made loads of mistakes." She listed a host of examples, among them was the size and height of the garden beds. At first, they made them too high and too wide. No one could reach the center without climbing onto the bed, which compacted the soil and inhibited growth. They had to rip all the beds apart and start over.

> We planted things, if they died, we planted something else. We were so stupid. We didn't even think about the climates of places. We [. . .] bought lavender from Norfolk, southeast coast. I brought it to wet cold Yorkshire. It died. And so, then we start to think, "Oh, yeah, we should look for stuff that grows here." So now we grow Yorkshire varieties of apples instead of Southern varieties of apples, because they do well here, they can stand the damp. It took us a few years to learn what we're doing.

Brown is not shy about admitting her mistakes. She takes pride in being "the fool that rushes in." Her seventy-five-year-old hindsight confirms that nothing bad has ever happened for doing so. "So, you fail," she said flatly, "You're no worse off." She gave an example:

> My husband and I have always rushed in, we ran away from London in 1973 to live off the land in Cornwall Borderland Farm, failed dismally, had to come back, go back to work. But we did it, we tried it [. . .] It's—I don't know—It's a kernel of craziness that's inside everybody that knows they should be doing something, and they've got all these other hang-ups that's stopping them from doing it.

It felt like she was talking directly to me. Perhaps she sensed my reverence for her public action; I've always had a crush on the daring. She went on to explain that children and old people are more likely to act on their "kernel of craziness" because they feel less inhibited by social expectations. She said it isn't until "people have got a young family, they start thinking 'well, what are they going to inherit?'" I thought about my one-year-old daughter asleep in an upstairs room. Brown was right. I want something better for my kids. I want the world to get its act together.

AS WORD GOT OUT about the gardens and people began to grasp the concept of food sharing, Brown and Clear thought up other ways for people to embody kindness. Ultimately their goal was to encourage people, as Brown puts it, "to look after each other, be kind to the planet, be kind to the environment, be kind to the town, be kind to wildlife, fairy people, real people, you know, you've just going to change the way of thinking about everything." It is not easy to change how people think. Kindness Corner is a good example of how people's perceptions of what it means to be kind can get in the way of their actually being kind.

Kindness Corner is literally a designated corner in the town where people can drop off items they no longer use. The goal was to divert them from going to the landfill and give them a second life with someone who needs them. "We're a small island," said Brown. "Our landfill sites [are] getting filled up, then what happens?" For her, the idea of Kindness Corner was straightforward. But just like the community gardens, it was difficult for people to grasp the concept at first. "They thought it was giving stuff to the poor and the needy and the homeless," she said. "A local dentist gave toothpaste, a local soap company gave soap, which is wonderful, but I had to keep enforcing the fact that it's anything that might be going to *waste.*" It turned out, people were confusing kindness with charity. Brown continued, "I've never been up to anyone [at Kindness Corner] and said, 'are you a poor person?' Because I don't really care whether they're poor people or not. It's there for everybody," she insisted. Eventually, people began to understand. A local restaurant donated two full size toasters and a panini press. Someone donated used bicycles. Another dropped off a baby stroller. The people of Todmorden were beginning to embrace kindness.

Surprisingly, kindness is what first got Brown and Clear into trouble. Even though they called their initiative Incredible Edible Todmorden, kindness had always been their brand. During my visit, I noticed the town was plastered with signs, stickers, and graffiti art of the word kindness. Brown explained how the signage got started, "We've always said you've got to be kind, but we never thought of putting the word anywhere." Then, for Clear's husband Fred's sixtieth birthday, Mary jokingly said that she wanted to give him the gift of kindness. Brown helped her make a sign spelling out the word in large white block capitals. "I stole the Hollywood font off of the internet," she recalled.

Brown and Clear had the word's eight enormous letters professionally printed and cut to give to Fred for his birthday. Each letter is around two meters tall. He put them up on the hillside by the supermarket in imitation of the famous Hollywood sign in Los Angeles. When locals saw the humongous sign declaring kindness, they wanted signs of their own. The print shop fulfilled hundreds of orders and the word kindness began popping up all over Todmorden in a variety of shapes and sizes.

So, this guy rings me up and says, "Is this Mrs. Brown speaking?" and I say "yes," not being quick enough to say who's asking. And he said to me "I am the Calderdale borough council's enforcement officer. What can you tell me about these illegal kindness signs that are springing up around town?" And I said, "They say kindness" and he said "Yes, but who put them up?" I said, "I don't know." "Well, what can you tell me about them?" I said, "Nothing! I don't know other than they say kindness." So, I said to him "I'll tell you what, I'll see what I can find out and I'll ring you back." That was over three years ago and I've never phoned him, but Calderdale borough council has made a film about themselves to show how wonderful they are, what a good local authority they are. And in their film has a kindness sign with them all standing in front of it. So, they decided they like it.

One of the reasons Brown gets away with her antics is because she's just so reasonable. Once people reflect on what she is asking of them, they realize it makes a lot of sense. A few years ago, the city built an expensive health center and surrounded it with what Brown calls corporate planting, mostly ornamental trees and bushes. "Nothing edible," Brown said with raised eyebrows. "And we said to them, 'Why would you build a health center and not surround it with healthy food? Why would people not see their five-a-day they're supposed to eat on the way in, and pick them on the way out?' They did a real Homer Simpson. 'Doh!,'" she said as she smacked her hand against her forehead. So, Brown and several volunteers got to work replacing holly and other prickly ornamental bushes with food—apple trees, nut trees, plum trees, cherry trees, raspberries, rhubarb, black currants, red currants, and white currants. They also planted an adjacent apothecary garden where they offer tutorials led by an herbalist who teaches people how to make tinctures and other holistic medicinal remedies.

ON A WALKING TOUR OF THE TOWN, Brown pointed out the apothecary garden and all the verdant, edible vegetation around the health center. We paused at a plum tree, plucked a slightly under ripened plum and tasted it. "These plum trees are quite interesting because Prince Charles was coming. And, oh, that was a joke in itself!" she exclaimed, signaling the start to another colorful story. Apparently about a year earlier, she and Clear began receiving phone calls from someone saying that Prince Charles wanted to do a tour of Incredible Edible Todmorden. As Brown tells it, "And we said, 'yeah, yeah, yeah.' I'm getting emails too. Delete, delete, delete. And then Mary got a letter from her letter box on Clarence House note paper, saying 'His Royal Highness, Prince Charles, Prince of Wales, wishes to come to an Incredible Edible tour.'" The letter was signed by the prince's equerry. The prince was, indeed, coming to Todmorden. When word got out, a company in Halifax that specializes in paving stones said they wanted to contribute something for the prince's visit. Clear and Brown requested plum trees. The Halifax company brought the plum trees to Todmorden and were not-so-coincidentally planting them on the day of the prince's tour.

For Brown, the Prince's visit was a nice surprise and provided a morale boost for the town. But she only offered the story as a footnote while introducing me to the plum tree. Her view of the world is so egalitarian that she couldn't care less whether she shared a bench with the Prince of Wales or a town drunk. Everyone is invited. Her egalitarianism combined with her gumption serves her well in getting her ideas off the ground.

In fact, within just six months of sewing their first seed, Incredible Edible Todmorden decided to host a harvest festival. It was not intended to be a provincial affair. "We were terribly arrogant," Brown said with a laugh referring to the fact that she sent a message to the famous chef Hugh Fearnley-Whittingstall, known for a popular television program called *River Cottage*. She invited him to come cook at the festival. "And he did! He came!" she exclaimed; eyebrows raised. Then she told a story about how the celebrity chef met one of Incredible Edibles' most ardent supporters.

> Okay, so we were growing herbs by the bus stop . . . there are only two places in Todmorden that are dry when it's raining—one's by the canal, the other one's the bus station. So, all the drunks and addicts hang out in these two places. So, [Feranley-Whittingstall's] there, picking herbs. A drunk with a cane in his hand rushed out and says, "Fuck off you, these are Todmorden's herbs and you can't have 'em." We had to say, "No, no, that's fine. He's cooking them for us. It's absolutely fine." We didn't know they even knew what we were doing or understand what we were doing. They not only understood, they were going to *defend* it.

In return, Brown defends them. A few years ago, she said, "the local council thought there were too many benches around town, undesirables are sitting on them and drinking. So, they took them away." She rolled her eyes and continued, "Well, we think it's good that people sit down here. If they're having a drink, they're having a conversation, you know? Our drunks are kind and nice people. They will talk to you as you go past, might embarrass you, but they're not aggressive."

In response to the council's decision, Brown and her gang began planting benches around town; metal ones bolted to the ground so they're hard to move. "They're really heavy," she said, and then described the difficulty she and the volunteers had moving the benches into place. Then two police officers came by, and Brown asked them for help. She said, "The police carried a bench, an *illegal* bench, and then sat on it to have their photographs taken." She sat back smiling with her hands on her knees, clearly pleased with herself. She told me that one of her tactics is to assume an air of authority whenever she is doing something illegal.

Not only does she do that, but she also invites the authorities to participate in the illegal activity. On our walking tour Brown pointed to a handrail under a bridge along the canal. It's a rope guide meant to assist pedestrians through the dark, wet underpass. "We weren't allowed to do it because it's a historic monument," she explained, "You aren't allowed to add anything to it. So, we did it, and then we got the mayor to come and cut the ribbon to open it." Brown describes a fundamental fearlessness at the heart of her public action that emboldens her. She said she is not afraid to make a fool of herself or, in her words, "not afraid to look like an idiot with a pink bucket on your head." But it's not always easy. Her ideas are not always welcome. And people can be quite cruel. "When somebody does have a pop and I say, 'Why am I doing this? I haven't even got children. So, what do I care if the world dies? When I'm dead, who cares?' But then I think, 'no, because you know, I love everybody, I love the animals. I love my friend's children and their children. So, the world has to continue.'" Not only should it continue, but it should be kind. And there is nothing passive about Brown's brand of kindness, either. It is as big and bold as the Hollywood sign.

HER INSISTENCE ON GOODWILL extends beyond the people in her community to include monopolistic, global corporations, as well. In 2015, she picked a fight with Walmart, owner of the supermarket chain Asda. Walmart bought property in Todmorden with plans to build an Asda supermarket. Construction began and then, for some reason, stopped. The site fell into disrepair and children were getting injured from climbing on the structures. Brown finally had enough. "It was ugly. It was right in the middle of our town, it was ruining our town," she said. And then continued:

> We said to the council, "Make them do something about it, please." Totally ignored. So, we thought, "Right, we'll fix it." We put up a huge placard out in front of the building that said "Asda are pants! If you

agree, Asda are pants, put your knickers on these clothes lines!"[5] We put two washing lines up. They were immediately filled with underwear. We rang up the BBC who came to film it and interviewed people in the street. "What do you think of Asda?" And they told them because they're very forthright here. It's Yorkshire. Before the end of the month, I had an email. "Dear Mrs. Brown, Worry not. We will knock the buildings down. We will put up fencing, garden-style fencing, and we will build you four raised beds. What size would you like?" So, Walmart did that, one of the most *hated* corporations in the world.

They also filled the brand-new railway sleeper garden beds with high quality gardening soil. In her recounting of the saga, Brown sounded just as surprised as I was to learn that she could make moral progress with a company famous for its mistreatment of workers, anti-union policies, reliance on foreign (and in some cases *child*) labor, and their general destruction of the planet and local economies.[6] She attributed her success with Walmart to her ingenuity, "You've got to think outside *several* boxes, not just outside one box." Brown and the people of Todmorden voiced their outrage with their underpants and were ultimately heard. Although a cynic might argue that Walmart's response was a drop in the bucket, it was enough of a response for people like Brown to create new ways to hold big corporations accountable.

The day after our interview was the third Sunday of the month. On my way out of town, while walking from the bed and breakfast to the train station, I saw volunteers of all ages, some of them wearing orange vests and nearly all of them carrying litter pickers, out on the sidewalks collecting cigarette butts and candy wrappers. There are approximately 300 volunteers who show up on the first and third Sunday of every month, rain or shine, to pick litter, weed garden beds, and sow seeds.[7] After they finish for the morning, they break bread together, congregating for a locally sourced, free-to-eat lunch donated by one of the neighborhood restaurants. This town is proof that there is value in bottom-up, inclusive power structures. They did not wait for leadership. They did not ask permission. They cultivated their own resources in each other. With the planting of a single seed, they slowly grew a community of kindness that has since dispersed around the world.

Reflection

Emotions can be elucidating and productive.[8] Even Aristotle, who you might imagine as a cold fish philosopher, emphasized emotions as central to our moral being and key to decision-making in public life.[9] Sometimes anger, sarcasm, and parody are appropriate ethical responses to a variety of situations. Social justice scholar Karen Tracy calls it "reasonable hostility," and, like Aristotle, argues that emotion can serve the needs of civil society.[10] Brown's passion was clear to me during our interview. She fumed over the fact that rich developers build golf courses instead of gardens in Sudan. She exhibited pride when she talked about Todmodern's designation as deprived. She expressed sadness and self-blame over being part of the throwaway society for so many years. And let's not forget her reasonable hostility toward Walmart's construction project. All these emotions, and more, were integral to Brown's civic engagement.

Passion fuels engagement and inspires creativity. In many ways, Brown exemplifies what Martin Luther King Jr. called "creative maladjustment." In two of his lesser-known speeches, one he delivered at Southern Methodist University in 1966 and one to the American Psychological Association in 1967, King resignifies the term "maladjustment." He said he understands the psychological application of the term and how it is good to live a well-adjusted life free of neuroses and other harmful mental health conditions, but he also said, "there are some things in our nation and the world to which I am proud to be maladjusted and wish all men of goodwill would be maladjusted until the good society is realized." He went on to list things to which he will never become "adjusted"— segregation and discrimination, religious bigotry, economic injustice, militarism, and physical violence. He finishes his thought with a call to action, "And so we need maladjusted men and women where these problems are concerned. It may well be that our whole world is in need of the formation of a new organization, the International Association for the Advancement of Creative Maladjustment." To give his audiences an idea of the types of people who would be part of this organization, he names historical figures who have demonstrated their creative maladjustment such as the prophet Amos, Abraham Lincoln, Thomas Jefferson, and Jesus Christ. For each figure he offers a quote to illustrate how they acted against injustice in their time calling on his audience (through refrain) to be "as maladjusted" as they were.[11]

During our interview Brown rattled off a list of things to which she is maladjusted, and ultimately recognized her ability to improve food scarcity in her town. Phronesis involves discerning whether and how we could be of benefit and then risking action toward that end. She said, "So, what can we do? Well, we can reach the bits of land we've got in front of us, take them, don't ask permission, just take them, and grow food on them." Her comment about not asking permission is in response to governmental apathy and inaction. She doesn't ask permission, but she also doesn't suffer any real consequences because Todmorden is a small community. Most people, including authorities, know Brown (at least by name) and understand the goals behind her misdemeanors. In other words, she enjoys the security of a social position that allows her to get away with it. That's important because not all of us are free to act up in that way.

The quality of Brown's playfulness, however, and her particular brand of creative maladjustment is something we might consider emulating. She doesn't take herself too seriously. Like the other people featured in this book, Brown's ego is well-checked. She readily admits to being "terribly arrogant" and making "loads of mistakes." And like the other stories we've read so far, Brown does everything she can to broaden participation. "If you eat, you're in," she says. That means everyone is invited and everyone can play. Police officers participate alongside so-called undesirables and even act, albeit un-wittingly, on their behalf.

Flipping the script on charity is another way Brown expands partici-pation. Like Lent (chapter 1), Brown recognizes how common conceptions of charity erect problematic and exclusionary boundaries about who is in a position to give and who is in a position to receive. From this perspective, poor people are imagined to be aliens and charity is a form of foreign trade, a way of sharing commerce without doing the work of inclusion. Brown's insistence on kindness disrupts the charity paradigm because kindness im-plies reciprocity. Everyone can give and everyone can receive.[12]

Brown's passion fuels her creativity and creativity is a guard against ad-justment because creativity is, by definition, imaginative. To be creatively maladjusted is to actively seek new responses to pressing problems. Nonvi-olent action is, of course, at the heart of King's definition of creative malad-justment. In the next chapter, you will meet two proponents of nonviolence, both inspired by King in different ways. One of them, Nawal Rajeh, explic-itly talks about how simple and uncreative a violent reaction is compared to the creativity inherent to peace. The chapter deepens our thinking about creativity by emphasizing process, context, constraints, and choice. It also echoes some of the themes we've touched on so far such as inclusion, pas-sion, risk, and maladjustment.

FIVE

Speak Up

Don't be afraid to just say what your idea is
and you'll find each other [. . .] when you speak that
vision aloud or that idea or that deep hope to
change the world aloud, you'll call people to you or
you'll be called to them.

—NAWAL RAJEH

We sat at a round table in the basement of the Enoch Pratt Free Library in Baltimore, a quiet, centrally located place for me to learn the story of Peace Camp from its creators Ralph Moore and Nawal Rajeh. Peace Camp is a free six-week summer camp for children ages 5–12 that teaches the principles of nonviolence.

Moore and Rajeh met fifteen years prior while Moore served as Community Program Director for St. Frances Academy. St. Frances is the oldest continually running Black Catholic school in the United States. Rajeh was there because The Jesuit Volunteer Corps (JVC), an organization that connects lay volunteers to underserved communities, assigned her to be Moore's assistant for a year. At the time, she was fresh out of college with a degree in political science and peace studies. Speaking about her placement with Moore at St. Frances, Rajeh smiled broadly and said, "The stars aligned." She and Moore looked at each other and laughed.

Despite their age difference (more than thirty years), Moore and Rajeh became fast friends. "We laugh a lot when we're together and we can joke. The world is a really grim place; it's just a friendship that centers me and helps me," said Rajeh. Moore's explanation for their shared outlook has to do with the closeness of their birthdays. "We found out we were like-minded, our birthdays are two days apart," he said by way of explanation. "It's true," Rajeh nodded in affirmation. They broke out in laughter again. Neither mentioned the 32-year-age difference.

Moore and Rajeh held their first Peace Camp in the summer of 2007. Rajeh encountered the idea in college—a one-week day camp focusing on inner peacebuilding skills. She asked Moore if he thought they could host something similar at St. Frances. He didn't see why not, and together they would host a free, six-week day camp at the St. Frances Academic Community Center in East Baltimore. Their idea was to create a fun, safe, and educational environment to get kids off the street during the idle summer months. As Moore explained it, "We decided to have a camp because I remember seeing kids jumping up and down on a dirty mattress and I said, 'Well that's going to be their summer, we can't do that. We got to do something, get them out of this heat.'" Moore's simple decisiveness called to mind a quote by French philosopher Jean-Paul Sartre about how we can't conceive of doing things differently until we decide that the current state of affairs is no longer tolerable.[1] I liked listening to Moore. He had no airs or pretenses. He spoke plainly and with a moral certitude that I could tell he had earned after more than six decades of living.

That first summer in 2003, seventy kids showed up for the day camp. Commenting on the extent of their ambition, Moore said there were two things driving everyone crazy in the beginning, "One was the length of time, and then *somebody* kept inviting the kids in, I mean if kids were showing up, we would say, 'Come on in.'" He raised his eyes to the ceiling and shook his head. Rajeh laughed and added, "We had a waitlist that was *not* a waitlist," meaning that Peace Camp accepted everyone. No one waited.

Peace Camp eventually found its groove.[2] Today it operates out of two sites, hosting as many as 110 kids at once. It is what Moore always wanted for the summertime mattress jumpers, "They eat breakfast, they eat lunch, they get snacks. They're in a safe environment and they get an opportunity to learn things," he said, adding, "I mean, the kids can be hard, you know. And for two summers, we didn't have decent air conditioning in either site. So *that*! *That* was hard." Hard as it may be at times, it would be much harder to turn someone away. Most of these kids wouldn't have other options for summertime enrichment. Moore described the significance of choosing St. Frances Academy as Peace Camp's original site, "We were nervous about the hail of bullets up and down the street in that neighborhood; the violence level was very high in that neighborhood, people being murdered in that neighborhood." The neighborhood to which Moore referred borders the Maryland State Penitentiary and the Baltimore City Jail. It is a tough place to be a kid. St. Frances Academy, where Peace Camp occurs, is a five-minute walk from the state pen.

Baltimore, in general, has a reputation for being hard. It is frequently at the top of national lists for homicide rates in cities with populations over 500,000. For young people, the statistics are particularly worrisome. Around the time Rajeh and Moore opened their first camp, The Baltimore City Health Department released research indicating that, on average each year over a five-year period, 27 youth (aged 0 to 17) were victims of homicide, 82 were victims of a non-fatal shooting, and 30 were arrested and convicted or adjudicated delinquent for murder or attempted murder. Sixty-two percent of the study's youth had a history of out of school suspension and/or expulsion.[3]

In addition to free meals, Peace Camp includes a weekly field trip; art, music, and cooking classes; yoga; and two weekly swimming lessons. Each summer, the camp honors a different peace hero such as Martin Luther King Jr., Shirley Chisholm, Harriet Tubman, or Colin Kaepernick. Campers study, write, and produce art about this person. The curriculum includes activities, games, and journal exercises related to the peace hero that emphasize self-respect, forgiveness, and communication. "I don't want to make it sound too melodramatic," said Moore, "but I think the things that we were trying to teach them could save their lives in some ways or save somebody else's life in the long run. I hate to think in such stark terms, but the violence is so real and so close, you know?"

MOORE HAS PERSONAL EXPERIENCE with what it's like to be a kid in Baltimore. He grew up on the West side of town in the Sandtown–Winchester neighborhood, the same one as Freddie Gray whose 2015 death in police custody became an important touchstone in the then-burgeoning Black Lives Matter movement.[4]

By the time Moore was eighteen years old, the United States had become deeply entrenched in Vietnam. All of his siblings—three brothers and a sister—joined the military. Two of his brothers served in Vietnam at the same time. "There's a picture of them shaking hands in one of the small villages," he told me. But when Moore received his own selective service number (a relatively low 57), he applied for conscientious objector status. The draft board denied his application because, in his view, he couldn't prove his sincerity. "You know," he said, "you're supposed to write a small treatise or something like Thomas Aquinas or something!" He shook his head in disbelief.

Moore was deeply opposed to America's war in Vietnam because he is fundamentally opposed to violence in general. He cited Martin Luther

King Jr. and Muhammad Ali's remarks against the war in Vietnam as early influences on his perspective. Another influence, he said, was Motown music. He spoke the lyrics to Edwin Starr's "War" the Temptations song "Ball of Confusion," and Freda Payne's "Bring the Boys Home." Fortunately, the war ended before Moore's number came up. And true to his ethos, he spent the entirety of his adult life in peaceful service to his community. He studied Social and Behavioral Sciences at The Johns Hopkins University and for the last three decades has tried to improve the circumstances for Baltimore's children. In addition to his work at the St. Frances Academy, he is program manager at a resource center for formerly homeless youth, a mentor coordinator for ex-offenders (who he refers to as potential achievers), and a volunteer for various poverty and unemployment programs around the city. He has always been inclined toward peace and justice even if he wasn't able to prove it to the draft board.

LIKE MOORE, Rajeh's proclivity toward peace began at a young age. Her parents left Lebanon in the late seventies before she was born. At the time, the country was steeped in a civil war that lasted from 1975–1990. Although she did not experience the pain of war first-hand, Rajeh learned about it while growing up in Youngstown, Ohio from her parents and other adults in her hometown's Arab community. In college she chose to study peace because, in her words:

> What could be more exciting than studying peace? This thing that is so mysterious and is so aligned with the human spirit and the amazing stories of what people do around the world when they decide that they want peace instead of war. It was just so exciting. It made my life so exciting, learning about these histories and movements.

Exciting as it was, her area of study was not very popular or at least not well understood by her classmates. Especially when the US invaded Iraq during her freshman year. "When I talked about peace or, 'oh I'm a peace studies minor,'" Rajeh recalled, "people you know, the reactions are like, 'oh, you know peace doesn't work' or like 'peace has never worked.'" They said things like "good luck finding a job." According to the National Center for Education Statistics, the most popular major today is business with nearly a quarter of US college students studying business, management, or marketing.[5] No wonder so much public discourse reflects zero-sum thinking.

Yet, instead of feeling dejected by her classmates' commentary and the US's global war on terror, Rajeh became more adamant that peace demanded deep study and attention. Convinced of the connection between peace and the human spirit, she wanted to learn how to cultivate it in others. "Military is strategic," she said. "It's a science, right? We've had military schools and academies forever. People research war and the military, but what about peace?" For Rajeh, the allure of peace is rooted in its elusiveness. "You're striving to know something that maybe can't yet be known, and yet it's so magnetic. It's so spiritual. It's so part of us." She continued:

> You read about Martin Luther King, like the courage that it takes. Where does that come from? Where does someone cultivate that? Whereas [in the military] you're trained to fight—they remove that thing in all of us that doesn't want to hurt each other. They just train it out of you [. . .] but what is it like to go the other way and say we're so powerful together? We're so creative together, right? I always thought with all of human creativity—*of course* we can create peace! It's the most creative part of us—is peace. And war? That's simple. That's like this thing we've just been told to do over and over.

The mystery and creativity inherent to peacemaking is ultimately what Peace Camp is all about. Practically speaking, the camps offer an alternative to the danger and hostility of the streets, providing a safe space for kids to learn how to interact peacefully. On another level it is an exploration into the peace process more broadly, seeking to *counter* violence by teaching young people how to become peaceful, actively engaged members of their community. As Moore explained. "We're trying to teach the kids how *not* to fight, and to teach them alternative behaviors and attitudes. And so, you have to understand that [. . .] if there was no fighting and no problems and no conflict, we really wouldn't need to exist."

Moore's point was that when you are a kid from a low-income neighborhood in Baltimore, being tough is always a safe bet. Both he and Rajeh understand the harsh reality their campers face every day. As Rajeh conveyed, "It's a hostile environment, I mean the city is hostile, school is hostile, the neighborhood is hostile, and you have to be really tough, I think, to grow up here. You have to have a lot of skills that help you be really tough." The challenge is convincing campers that toughness is not the only way forward. Rajeh continued:

> We want the kids to be kids. So, you know, if you get to come here and be a kid, that's huge for us. If that's the [. . .] thing that one child took from this, then that's a win. And for me, I don't want to—I was a really

soft kid, you know, kind of tender—I don't want to make them me because I don't think I could have grew up or survived in a lot of ways in Baltimore, but could you be like, could you be just soft enough that you get to let your guard down in the space here, when we're together? Could we create a community where you get to come in and make friends and not be scared and not have to be tough all the time and not be bullied either?

I liked Rajeh's phrasing, "just soft enough," and her recognition that she understands the constraints of the culture. Because she didn't grow up in a neighborhood like the one she works in, she didn't develop the same attitudes, values, and beliefs. She doesn't want the campers to be like her, but she wants them to see alternative modes of engagement. Toward that end, each summer the campers study the biography and activism of a famous peace hero.

One year the camp's peace hero was Nelson Mandela, who was still alive at the time. "The children asked me if I could reach Nelson Mandela on the telephone," Moore grinned. He tried calling the South African Embassy but was unable to reach Mandela directly. Because Mandela's birthday is in the summertime, the camp had a big cake, and the kids sang Happy Birthday. The children liked learning about present-day peace heroes as opposed to historical figures. It made the people more accessible, their actions more achievable, and the idea of peace more possible.

To bring peace even closer to home, Moore and Rajeh started focusing on local peace heroes. For example, in 2018 the camp's peace hero was Erricka Bridgeford who was leading Baltimore's ceasefire movement. Another year it was President Obama's special advisor on green jobs, Anthony Kapel "Van" Jones. The kids took a field trip to DC to deliver a little peace tree. While they were there, they visited the Lincoln Memorial, where Martin Luther King Jr. gave his famous address. "The kids enjoyed, I think, standing at that spot because it's clearly marked, and they could feel something," said Moore. He didn't elaborate on what he thought the campers might have felt, but in response to their obvious enthusiasm for activism, Peace Camp expanded its curriculum.

Now, in addition to interpersonal peacekeeping, campers learn the tactics of community organizers and social justice advocates. "We're trying to find a path where our kids learn to be organizers . . . and be more involved with the larger movements that are happening in Baltimore," Rajeh explained. She gave an example from the most recent summer when campers met with housing organizers from United Workers in Baltimore.

Rajeh's favorite story, however, is about how the campers organized to keep East Baltimore's neighborhood pool open. "There's a walk-to pool right by Saint Frances," she explained, "and for three years in a row it got slated to be cut from the budget." The campers wrote letters and staged a protest. Television and radio news crews covered the event. "One year . . . someone from the [Baltimore] Ravens marketing staff heard about them and called Moore and said, 'how much would it cost to keep all the pools open? Not just *that* pool.'" Rajeh's eyes and her smile widened. Moore made some calls, did some math, learned the number, and reported back to the inquiring Raven's staff member. That summer, the NFL team covered the cost to keep all of the city pools open for business.

In response to their consistent activism, advocacy, and (let's face it) publicity, Baltimore's Director of Recreation and Parks invited the campers to his office. This story lit up Rajeh's face. She leaned forward in her chair and swallowed fits of laughter as she told me the story:

> And so, they're sitting in these chairs and what I remember most is that like, the really little kids—their feet don't touch the floor, right?—so they're like swinging around in the chairs and having a great time, and the Director gives them this like really clearly-prepared analysis of, you know, "if your mom gives you x amount of lunch money and then you go to school and this is how much this combination of things costs, then what happens? It's like okay, you can't afford that thing. So, that's what's happened here at the city." And so, he's trying to explain that that's why the budget had gotten cut [and the pools closed] and so when he was all done giving this explanation, he said, "Now are there any questions?" And one of our five-year-olds who's sitting with his little Chuck Taylors up and had been swinging the whole time raised his hand. "Yes, young man?" and he says, "Why are you closing the pool?"

All three of us laughed at the camper's charm. Five years old and already speaking truth to power.

LIKE THE CITY'S BUDGET for neighborhood pools, funding for Peace Camp (which comes in the form of grants and donations) is not always a guarantee. In 2012, ten days before the start of camp, Rajeh learned that their funding had been cut. The kids had already enrolled and were looking forward to seeing their camp friends again. Rajeh could not bear telling them that Peace Camp would be canceled. Showing up mattered to these kids.

Within weeks, Rajeh applied for grants and scraped together funds. By mid-summer she was able to cobble together enough money to take them on a one-week camping trip in Shenandoah. The kids were overjoyed. They had resigned themselves to a summer without Peace Camp. Receiving an invitation for an overnight field trip was a thrill. "It was great," she said. "We did that trip again the next year just because everyone loved it." In order to have more control over their funds, Moore and Rajeh set up a nonprofit called By Peaceful Means with the slogan "Reviving the heartbeat of the community." When I asked Rajeh what the heartbeat meant, she described it as an aliveness, an ability to be creative, dynamic, and fun. She said:

> Violence—structural violence, physical violence—is the opposite of that. It keeps us afraid or keeps us stagnant or alone or isolated. So, I think the heartbeat is peace. It's saying let's be alive together, let's enjoy life together, let's change the situation together. Let's transform ourselves and transform the community.

Rajeh believes strongly in people's ability to collaborate for positive change. In her words:

> Don't be afraid to just say what your idea is and you'll find each other. I think that peacemakers find each other, and when you speak that vision aloud or that idea or that deep hope to change the world aloud, you'll call people to you or you'll be called to them.

In many ways her story is a testament to that belief. Her year-long volunteer assignment to be Moore's assistant landed her where she is now and has been for the past fifteen-plus years. In 2010 the camp changed its name to reflect her efforts—The Nawal Rajeh Peace Camp.

Since its inaugural summer, Peace Camp has been a moving target and a learning process. Moore and Rajeh have maintained a collaborative open playbook, reflecting Moore's personal philosophy of "absolute rigidity in planning and absolute flexibility in execution." Just as their own humility keeps them open to change and possibility, they also do not expect campers to arrive ready to embody peace. Peace Camp is a training ground. As Rajeh explains, "The curriculum is based on *cultivating* inner peace . . . It's not just that some people are born peaceful, and some people aren't—You're *training.*" At Peace Camp, training begins by asserting the campers' personal significance and self-worth. It is the opposite of military-style boot camps, which strip recruits of their identity and self-esteem. At Peace Camp, everyone has merit, and everyone is worthy of dignity.

The camp, as a whole, practices a form of radical inclusivity uncommon to other social institutions. Rajeh is adamant that no one should be removed from Peace Camp under any circumstances. Expulsion forecloses opportunities for growth. As Rajeh explained, "When you fight in school you just get suspended or expelled. There's no learning around how to deal with those emotions." When kids fight at Peace Camp, it is a learning opportunity and a chance to practice peace. Rajeh gave an example of their approach:

> We've had kids sitting in a room together, you know across the table and they couldn't leave until they had drawn like four things that they both enjoyed and what we've seen over the years is, you know, they're fighting in the morning, and the next day they're friends. [laughs]

Day-to-day small-scale victories like these are validating, but because Peace Camp only occurs a few weeks out of the year, Moore and Rajeh recognize that their influence is only ever marginal. Parents and guardians have a much greater sphere of influence through sheer exposure. It's critical they buy in to what Peace Camp is trying to do.

Yet one of the biggest challenges Moore and Rajeh face is earning parental trust. "In the beginning we had a lot of pushback from parents," explained Moore, "They came to the program, I think, because it was free, but they really pushed back on a lot of the things." The central concern among parents was that Peace Camp would teach their children to be weak or passive. Parents worried that their children would be bullied or treated like doormats. According to Moore, "Some parents tell their kids to fight, you know, and it's because they don't want their kids to be bullied. So, they tell them, 'If you don't fight, I'm going to fight you when you get home.' So, the kid is set up in this God-awful situation."

But pacifism is not passivism. That is, while pacifists are peace loving, they are not pushovers. It is an active stance of resistance against violence and injustice. Some of the most famous pacifists were hot-headed. There's nothing inherently wrong with anger. Or in Moore's words, "It's okay to be angry. The Lord Jesus was angry." The trick is finding a way to sit with anger, question its warrant, and channel it productively. Rajeh added on with a story about how sometimes Peace Camp's learning objectives inadvertently reach parents as well.

As Rajeh told it, a few years ago on the first day of Peace Camp, a young boy hit a young girl on the playground. No one notified the counselors nor the camp directors. Instead, the girl used her cell phone to call her father.

The girl's father arrived at camp, found Rajeh and demanded to know why the camp had not notified him. Rajeh admitted that she was unaware of the incident. The father was fuming and wanted to speak to the young man, which Rajeh explained is not an option. "It's one of our no-nos," she said, "We never let a parent speak to a child without that other [child's] parent present." Instead, Rajeh invited the angry father to a meeting with the boy's mother later that day. Rajeh continued:

> So, we have the parent meeting and we do all the things that we nor-mally do, which is Ralph [Moore] talks about why is it so important, what are the messages out there, what are we trying to do, and then he asks the parents to be partners with us, basically, and ask the kids what's going on and, you know, learn with us. And then I did the thing that I usually do, which is talk about how we operate under what we call "restorative practices," [. . .] which is [not] what happens when your kids fight in school—they're suspended, they're expelled. And I talked about how we don't remove anyone from our community, that we all belong here and that we won't kind of discard or throw anyone away, and that we're going to work together to counterprogram and to build something new and different together in this environment. So, that happens. Then we have a conversation, and the mother of that son was so embarrassed about what had happened that she's like, "He's not com-ing back here anymore. You don't even have to worry; he's not coming back here." And the father who had just been so upset, [. . .] maybe an hour before said, "No, no, no. I don't want that to happen. [If] this is a restorative place then let's talk about what we could do, and how we can work together. I want him to be here."

The boy wasn't in camp the next day. Worried, Rajeh called the house. His mother explained that he was missing the day as punishment. Rajeh smiled as she remembered the phone call. "It was so great because she laughed as she said, 'I knew that you all were going to call me. I promise we'll be back tomorrow.' And *he did*! He did come back, and he grew *a lot!*" Rajeh beamed.

Peace Camp is a feat of social engineering. The mother's response, "I knew that you all were going to call," reflects an unprecedented expectation of care. Through dogged consistency, Moore and Rajeh built a social infra-structure where none previously existed. And the ethic of care extends both ways. Now, Moore and Rajeh enjoy the support of families and commu-nity donors alike. These days Peace Camp not only has a reliable source of funding, but it also has reliable staffing. Previous campers become teenage counselors. They benefited from Peace Camp themselves and can handle and de-escalate squabbles among the campers with proficiency. Plus, teenagers are cool. They carry social capital among youngsters that goes a long way. "They're in high school," said Rajeh, "the little kids look up to them."

When Rajeh first proposed the idea for a camp, the notion of its longevity did not occur to her. She did not anticipate being able to watch the campers grow up. That was not part of her imagination then. It couldn't have been. Yet, she says, that it has been the biggest reward, "You can see a kid who had a really big anger problem a few years ago is now dealing with their issues differently." Moore acknowledges these advances with slightly less awe, as if he never doubted the campers' potential. For him, it's just another indication that peace, nonviolence, is the only way to be in the world. "We have to just keep being a witness for the peace side," he said, "and keep organizing and pushing and emphasizing that it's about saving the children." His comment reminded me of Martin Luther King Jr.'s words in his final 1968 Mountaintop speech—"it's nonviolence or nonexistence."[6]

Reflection

The practical aspect of phronesis has to do with responding to the particulars of a concrete reality. This chapter highlights the significance of place and localization. East Baltimore is a very specific setting for Moore and Rajeh's intervention. Moore grew up and eventually returned to work in the very same neighborhood. His history with the place, his deep understanding of its culture allowed him to see where he could be of benefit. He understood his fit in terms of power and positionality. By contrast, Rajeh came from a different place and background. She arrived in East Baltimore with the beneficial qualities of a stranger—she had an outside perspective with formal training in conflict transformation, yet her humility and respect for the local order kept her from trying to impose her ideas on anyone. Connecting with Moore and his tacit knowledge of East Baltimore as well as spending time in the community allowed Rajeh to understand the specificity of the needs there. She floated the idea for a summer camp to Moore and it made sense. Together, they built Peace Camp right there, in the center of the neighborhood, in the center of the need.

Phronesis is developed through habit. In other words, doing the right thing in the right place, at the right time, in the right way, and for the right reason is usually the result of a series of other choices that person made. Rajah made an unconventional choice by studying peace in college. She made another one by signing up for a year of volunteering after graduation. Same with Moore, who opposed the war in Vietnam even as his two brothers were off fighting it. Choices like these are significant because they resist the pull of social gravity and cultural inertia. To some, they seem like a risk because we tend to infer a direct relationship between obedience and security. But for Rajeh and Moore, the bigger risk is akrasia—not listening to what they know is right. When Moore saw kids jumping up and down on an old mattress, he said to Rajeh, "Well that's going to be their summer, we can't do that. We got to do something." Feeling the need to do something is to feel the pull of what Aristotle called "telos."

Telos translates as the end, or completion and undergirds all forms of activity. You can think of telos as the ultimate object, aim, or goal.[7] For example, the telos of an acorn is to become an Oak. The telos of business is to accumulate wealth. And, according to Aristotle, the telos of phronesis is to bring about the good society, which he describes as social wellbeing for all.[8] For Rajeh, the idea of peace always felt magnetic, like a pull. In my mind, that feeling must be the tug of phronesis's telos asking her to turn her moral instincts into practical action. Other chapters referenced a similar phenomenon. Romjue described our heart's "resonant frequencies" (chapter 2), Bromberg said it was our "shared humanity" (chapter 3), and Brown called it "the kernel of craziness" that exists in all of us (chapter 4). What they, including Aristotle, seem to be describing is a calling.

In his lectures and writing, philosopher-activist Cornel West, frequently uses a version of the line, "justice is what love looks like in public" and argues that peace, justice, and love should be our human calling. Speaking at Harvard's divinity school in 2017, West urged his audience to consider what kind of person they want to be and what kind of life they want to live. In his words:

> After critical reflection, after the analytical understandings of the operations of power and structures of domination and oppression—you say, "This is the kind of human being I choose to be before the worms get my body." That's a vocational question, not a professional one, a question of calling, not just your career, a question of life and death, not just your upward mobility in terms of your status.

West distinguishes vocation from profession, calling from career, labor from work. Our profession, our work, is something we do for money. We clock in and we clock out. Labor, by contrast, sets its own pace. We might get paid for our labor, but it is harder to quantify. Moore and Rajeh named several rewards, none of which were money. The choices they made reflect vocational, life or death questions, rather than career or status questions. Those choices, as West points out, stem from a careful process of discernment. "After critical reflection, after analytical understanding," he said. West's emphasis on critical reflection and analysis connects to our definition of phronesis as the capacity to discern a practical course of action. Hearing the call comes first, the choices follow.

In the next chapter you meet Shannon Keith, a woman who is deeply moved by the telos of phronesis. Her formal education is in business, but her line of questioning is almost exclusively vocational. She is a resolute bushwhacker when it comes to charting paths toward Aristotle's good society. Her story raises questions about confidence and risk and how we might apply a business model to doing good. Something else I learned from Keith is that it's not enough to champion a cause, you need to be your own champion as well. Especially when the going gets tough—Be in your own corner.

SIX

Take Risks

We're learning and stumbling and
failing all along the way, but I feel like
we're at least trying, you know?

—SHANNON KEITH

I bought my first pair of punjammies as a graduate student. My roommate headed the local chapter of Association for India's Development (AID) and she recommended that I check out this company called Sudara. The company's website was pretty bare bones at the time. It explained how the non-profit existed to offer vocational training for women to escape sex trafficking in India. The page showed about eight photos of different colored pajama pants that were sewn by those women with a disclaimer that proceeds would go back into the nonprofit to support the cause. I bought three pairs—one for myself, my mother, and sister-in-law. More than ten years later, I still wear mine. The cotton has thinned but the colors remain vibrant.

Visiting the Sudara webpage today, it looks like a high fashion e-commerce website. A banner at the top announces ongoing sales. Bright photos of professional models wearing colorful robes, tops, shorts, and, of course, pajama pants dominate the main page. Tabs direct customers to different categories of merchandise for women, men, kids, even dog bandanas and face masks. In the last ten years Sudara has expanded from a nonprofit focused on vocational training into a certified benefit corporation (B-Corp) with vocational centers across India that pay above average wages and offer healthcare, a pension, counseling, and childcare assistance.

I spoke to Sudara's founder and CEO, Shannon Keith, in 2019 from Sudara's headquarters in Bend, Oregon. She was in the middle of liquidating all the warehouse inventory in preparation for the company's official transfer to India. She was calling the liquidation sale "India or Bust." The warehouse was an absolute riot of color, pattern, and texture. Delicate metallic threads wove their way through tasseled fabrics the color of ocean, sky, and sunset. I was both excited and nervous to speak with Keith. I had been following her progress for some time. It helped to learn that she, too, was feeling nervous. Not because of me, of course, but because she was preparing for Sudara's official move from Oregon to India.

There is an intensity to Keith, a sense of urgency and impatience. She speaks quickly, uses emphatic gestures, and her voice has a punch to it; I felt myself scooch forward in my seat. This wasn't going to be a casual, armchair kind of conversation. Keith was all business. Although the problems she confronts are not small ones—sex trafficking and slave labor—she speaks with such ferocity and certitude, like a coach giving a locker room speech at halftime, it made me want to get out there and grab the world by its shirt collar. By the end of our conversation, I was fired up and feeling a little embarrassed that I hadn't been more proactive. "It's not rocket science," she said flatly about her own journey with Sudara. In her mind, she simply responds to needs as she encounters them.

SUDARA'S ORIGIN STORY began in 2005 during Keith's second trip to India. She found herself standing in front of a group of women and children giving a short speech in dedication of a freshwater well that her family donated to a community in Andhra Pradesh. She learned about the country's water insecurity during her first trip there the year before. She donated funds for the well in lieu of giving a gift to her mother and father-in-law for their 40th wedding anniversary. They accompanied her on the trip in 2005, eager to meet the faces of the community members who would benefit from the well donation. Everyone was surprised, least of all Keith, that she would be giving a speech. "Normally they would have asked my husband as the man in a very patriarchal society, but since it's all these women, they were like, 'oh maybe it's more appropriate if a woman in the family addresses the crowd,'" she explained.

The reason the crowd consisted mostly of women was because Keith was standing in front of a brothel in one of India's many red-light districts. After her family donated money for the well to a local NGO, the NGO assigned well construction to a community in need by drawing from a re-cipient list. The process is similar to how we think about organ donation. There is a lot of Kismet involved. This case was particularly serendipitous because Keith is a dogged social justice advocate. Connecting her, of all people, to the brothel and then positioning her to deliver a speech in front of the women who lived there meant Keith was about to set her sights on a new campaign—human trafficking.

Prior to the well dedication ceremony, Keith was relatively unaware of the extent of India's sex trade. Prostitution laws in India are vague, opening the door to sinister human trafficking practices. Most of India's trafficking problem is internal and involves women and girls from the most disadvantaged social strata, but women and girls from outside of India—China, Japan, Thailand, Sri Lanka, Afghanistan—have been found to be working as prostitutes in India as well.[1] According to a 2018 report written by the US Department of State, thousands of unregulated work placement agencies lure adults and children into sex trafficking under false promises of employment, subjecting some women and girls to both forms of slavery—labor and sex.[2]

Traffickers increasingly use websites, mobile applications, and online money transfers to facilitate commercial sex. An increasing global awareness of sex trafficking in India has led to brothels becoming the targets for rescue missions and criminal investigations. Yet, in response, women and children are being forced to endure sexual abuse in small hotels, vehicles, huts, and private residences. On top of that, in exchange for money and services, corrupt law enforcement officers warn traffickers about intended rescue efforts.

Keith learned about these circumstances in 2005 when she met the recipients of her family's well donation. Her response was outrage; first at the reality of it, and second at the fact that she had only just learned about it.

> I became completely shattered by what I discovered was one of the most horrifying social injustices of our time. And at the time—this was 15 years ago—nobody's talking about human trafficking. Nobody's talking about sex trafficking, nobody even knows what that means. Most of the people I experienced when I came back to the US think I'm exaggerating or sensationalizing or making this stuff up. I was like, "absolutely not—I saw with my own eyes." You know, why would I make something up? I have no reason to do that.

Within a year, Keith partnered with a sewing center in India to hire and teach six women, who escaped the sex trade, to sew a pattern for pajama pants. Her idea was to create an economic alternative for women prone to sex trafficking by offering a safe space for them to learn the skills necessary to become seamstresses. Once they were able to successfully sew pajama pants, Keith posted the pants for purchase online. Any proceeds would go back into her fledgling social enterprise.

The clean simplicity of the idea belies its ingeniousness. When I asked Keith how she came up with the plan, she shrugged and chalked it up to the cosmos.

> Honestly, [. . .] I wish I could take the credit, but I feel like it was divine inspiration, because I didn't think about it. It literally just came to me. And I would love to be able to take credit if I was like, "ooh, I went through all these options and I came up with this brilliant solution," but it wasn't like that. It was just like, oh—it popped into my head.

Her epiphany happened while she was standing in front of the women at the brothel in Andra Pradesh to give her speech about the freshwater well. Her chest tightened as she looked out at them. She had just learned about the cruel reality of their situation and there they were looking back at her. She said they looked so beautiful sitting in vibrantly colored swaths of cotton fabric twisted and draped over their bodies. That's when she said the idea came to her "in a flash"— women's pajamas.

> I didn't come home and metabolize and think about it. It literally came to me in a flash of inspiration—*women's pajamas*. Like, duh. Boom. Like, as I'm speaking to them. I didn't go "Oh, I want to help them, how should I help? Let me do this, let me run it through a rubric"—I didn't do any of that. It was really like *women's pajamas*. I was like, "Whoa, okay, where did that come from? God? Okay, great. Let's see if this works."

On the plane ride home, Keith got out a notebook and let her mind mull over the notion of women's pajamas. It actually made a lot of sense. Pajamas aren't fashion sensitive nor are they especially difficult to sew. "We're not talking couture gowns here," she said. Besides, most people own at least one pair of pajamas. "Even if you sleep naked," said Keith, "you have to put on something to get your coffee in the morning." Although it seemed like a good idea, one that checked many of the boxes on her figurative rubric, she did not want to assume it would work or even that her help would be welcome. Keith is nothing if not pragmatic.

WHEN SHE GOT HOME, she dug out her sewing machine. She had only used it once before to sew a pair of curtains and was by no means an expert. She bought some cheap cotton fabric and began making samples. She figured that if pajamas were easy enough for her to sew, they would be easy enough for other women who also knew little about sewing. Once she completed a few samples, she conducted some informal market research by asking her online social network whether they would buy the pajama pants and for how much.

At the same time, she was researching potential partners in India. What local groups were interested in helping victimized women? Her only point of contact was the NGO who installed the freshwater well. She didn't know anyone who helped women out of brothels. Through incessant internet searching she found an organization in Mumbai that helped women leave brothels through job creation. One of their vocational training options was sewing.

> I was like, "hey bingo!" this crosses a lot of the things that I was already thinking about. So, I went to India and [. . .] pitched my idea. Now, they could have said a flat "No, thanks, not interested. We don't need your American idea, scram," you know, and then I would have been like "Okay fair enough," you know, like I guess [. . .] it isn't gonna work or whatever, but thankfully that wasn't the case.

Evidently the organization that was teaching women to sew did not have a broad market for their products, meaning the women could only sew things that would sell locally, for example, school uniforms. The organization told Keith that if she could bring a market, they would be enthusiastic about a partnership. "So that was an early win," Keith recalled, "They're saying yes, they want and need this sort of help. We're not shoving it on them, not forcing it down their throat . . . We're just open-handed like, 'Hey, would this be helpful?' They're like, 'Yes, it would.' Oh, yay! Perfect. Awesome. Let us work together."

Keith is wary of her positionality—she referred to her whiteness and nationality more than once—and, somewhat ironically (given her business model), she detests consumerism more than anyone I have ever met. Let us not forget that she bought her in-laws a freshwater well for their anniversary. Yet, she figured out a way to make consumerism work for her. She recognizes that consumption (on some level) is necessary (i.e., you need pajamas even if you sleep naked). She explained using M&Ms as an analogy for money:

> We're not saying spend more money. We're not advocating to spend more. We're saying—you have this amount you're already spending— choose to shift that, shift your M&Ms so that, whether there's a ton of M&Ms or just a handful of M&Ms, those M&Ms are going to a good supply chain. And those M&Ms are not causing greater harm.

When consumers buy pajamas from Keith as opposed to other retailers, they receive not only a beautiful product, but also the satisfaction that their money is being put to good use. For Keith, it is about reimagining how retail could work; consumerism with a conscience. Keith's perspective is backed by scholarship in anthropology that views consumption as a series of rituals, in which material goods play a role in forming social relationships.[3]

For Keith, ethical consumerism is more impactful than rote charity because it's a relationship of reciprocal exchange that assumes a level of equity and respect.

> These women don't need Toms shoes to like give their kids free shoes. They need a job so that they can buy their own kid's shoes. You know, that's a game changer. Giving free stuff and charity actually more often than not is just a way to make the rich feel like they're doing good. It doesn't really help the poor.

After receiving a green light from her sewing center partner in India, Keith quit a steady and well-paying job in corporate America to start her own company. She called it Sudara, a made-up word based on the Sanskrit word Sundara, meaning "beautiful." Wordplay was necessary to secure a domain name and establish a web presence.

> We just remove the n and it's Sudara, but it's a riff and sort of an ode to that word which means beautiful [. . .] because we feel like these women are beautiful, the textiles are beautiful, our garments are beautiful. There's nothing more beautiful than freedom and dignity, which is what every human being should have access to.

Almost ten years after delivering her speech in dedication of the freshwater well, Sudara became a for-profit benefit corporation in 2015 and Keith launched a non-profit subsidiary called Sudara Freedom Fund. The sole purpose of the non-profit is to help women and their children gain access to education, housing, and micro-loans. The impetus for expanding beyond job creation was the recognition that jobs, while essential, weren't quite enough aid for these women. Keith wanted to offer more support.

> At the end of the day, sure, we can all feel sorry for these ladies and cry our eyes out at how horribly sad it is, which I've done my fair share of that too. But at the end of the day that doesn't help them, nor does just throwing money at them help them. What they need is a job. If they're not going to sell their bodies, what are they going to do? Right? So

that was the basic essence, but they need a lot of other things too. They need wraparound services. They need counseling. They've been severely sexually traumatized; they need medical care. They need help with their children.

Keith knows it's not realistic for her to be the only entity offering these services, but she is motivated to at least try. Part of her motivation stems from what she perceives as public apathy and an unwillingness to be inconvenienced. "If people consider only what's possible," she said, "we just stay with the status quo and there's no innovation. There's no anything. Because I can tell you, this work is damn hard." She went on to say that it's easy, in this line of work, to become myopic and how critical it is to have a support system.

> [N]obody's helping these women, nobody even cares, all people care about is getting cheap shit at Walmart. [Laughs.] Like, that's all they care about. So, how are we [Sudara]—this little voice in the wilderness—supposed to change anything, you know? And in those moments, we just sort of remind each other, "Well, hey, at least we have each other, and we have our awesome friends in India, and we are making a difference." And so, if I'm feeling a moment of overwhelm and discouragement, one of my teammates is like, "What? Hey! Snap out of it! Yeah, it sucks. But look at all these amazing things, look at these women and children [. . .] their life has been transformed, you know? They matter. Like even though we're not affecting the millions yet, we're affecting these 200. That's awesome!" "Oh, yeah, that's right. That *is* awesome. Okay, back at it!"

Compassion fatigue is real. But Keith keeps her focus on generating equity, understanding that, in her words, "it's the path of hardest resistance, but it's worth it." The reason equity is so challenging is because it involves distributing resources based on the needs of recipients. It requires careful attention and deep listening to give people the resources and opportunities they need to flourish. Often, we confuse equity with equality, but they are significantly different in their approach. Equality focuses on fairness through sameness, giving people the same opportunities and resources. Equality can only work if everyone starts from the same place and needs the same things. By contrast, equity recognizes that everyone has unique circumstances and unique needs.

Promoting equity requires constant reflection and context-based decision making. That is, in part, why Keith decided to move Sudara Incorporated fulltime to India, to help facilitate upward mobility within the corporation. Sewing pajama pants was always meant to be "a first job out of the brothels," Keith explained. What she wants to see is some sort of profit sharing potential but isn't quite sure what that could look like or even if the women would be interested in it. "Would that be meaningful for a woman to own shares in a company? I don't know, maybe, maybe not, so let's have discussions and talk with her," mused Keith. She continued, "But either way, we need an Indian entity to be able to distribute equity all the way down the supply chain." Keith is careful to consult the women she supports at every turn. Her goal is not to rescue, but to offer access and opportunity. "It's not forcing anyone to do anything, it's giving them a choice." Some women choose to stay in the brothels. For a variety of reasons, they are unwilling or unable to leave. Keith respects that choice and communicates that the Sudara door will always remain open. One way she does this is by partnering with other nonprofits in the community to ensure that women get the type of assistance that they feel willing to accept. She used the analogy of an addict to explain:

> When you say "Hey, do you want to go to rehab?" They're not all like "Oh, yeah. I've been just waiting for you to take me. Thank you so much!" [It] isn't that story all the time. So, it's kind of the same [. . .] they have lots of other issues, they're not always like "Yeah sure, you're offering me a different job. Awesome, I've just waited for you to come along." You know, but a lot of times they'll say "I'm not ready to leave right now, but I don't want my kids growing up in this, and I don't want my daughter to become, you know, in this lifestyle. So, I'm willing to like, have you take my kids and give them a better life."

Local nonprofit partners offer what Keith described as semi-orphan homes where children of women in the brothels can live and have access to life-sustaining resources.

THE FRAGILE AND FLEDGLING network of care Keith worked to establish in order to serve these women was not "rocket science," as she said. It is difficult and energy-draining work but "it isn't somebody else's problem to fix," she said. "It's *all of our* problems. *We* are the problem." She continued:

> People have to be able to look at themselves in the mirror and say, "I'm the problem." Blame Donald Trump all you want, I hate the guy and didn't vote for him myself, but he's not the problem with the world. The

world was screwed up before he came to office, you know? So again, human beings want to always shift the blame, and until they're willing to take a good hard look in the mirror, nothing's gonna change [. . .] But at the end of the day, you can lead a horse to water, but you can't make it drink. So, they have to have an enlightenment, and they have to take the facts and not just brush it off as like, "Oh, no, that's someone else's problem. I can't do that. I'm busy, I'm a soccer mom. I have kids to raise." Yeah. So, do I. You don't get a moral pass.

Keith becomes indignant around the subject of an apparent bourgeois nonchalance. Yet she is convinced that the very habit she despises the most—consumerism—can also be our saving grace, "You vote with your dollars. This isn't a communist bloc. On our shelves, you have things that are made by slaves and you have things that aren't. And you're the one keeping the slaves employed because you're buying their stuff. Nobody wants to swallow that pill but that's the truth." In response to pushback that consumers can't afford to make the moral choice, or that they are uninformed about slave labor she said:

> There's always a workaround. So, no, you don't have to shop at Whole Foods, but you can go to your farmer's market and you can grow your own garden—equally organic. And you're actually saving pennies, so you're smarter. No, you can't afford to shop at fill-in-the-blank [. . .] but you *can* afford to shop at Goodwill, where you're not putting more inputs in. [. . .] So, you don't get a pass if you're a college student and you're on a fixed income. You don't get a pass if you're that family of four on only $40,000 that lives in Arkansas. Sorry, you don't get the pass, because it's not just rich people who are the only ones who can afford to do good.

Keith's impatience for excuses is both intimidating and laudable. It is hard for her to understand, let alone accept, willful ignorance. It is antithetical to her modus operandi. She moves through the world deliberately and allows herself to be affected along the way. And once she has been affected, she cannot help but get involved.

Her approach reminds me of a style of breath meditation called tonglen, which loosely translates as taking and sending. The idea is to reverse our impulse to seek pleasure and avoid suffering. For example, when someone tells you to take a deep breath, the underlying assumption is that you are breathing in peace and tranquility and breathing out stress and affliction. In tonglen breath meditation, however, you do the opposite— breathe in pain and sorrow and breathe out peace and relief. It is an exercise in compassion and selflessness. It takes courage to draw pain into your heart, transform it, then release it back out again. The day Keith got up to speak in front of those women about the freshwater well in Andhra Pradesh, she took her first deep breath and the last twenty years have evinced a series of healing exhales.

Spirited dedication aside, Keith readily admits that she doesn't always have the answers. The company's move to India is a good example. Equity sharing is new to Keith, and it is relatively new to existing business models. But complex problems require a different type of thinking. "There's no silver bullet—that's not how life works," she said with a laugh, "And we don't have it all figured out but like we're committed to making progress and getting better." In addition to positively impacting the lives of women and children in India, Keith also wants to make waves in corporate America. Her goal is to prove that accountability can be profitable.

> I mean we're learning and stumbling and failing all along the way, but
> I feel like we're at least trying, you know? We get a lot of flak for not
> doing it perfectly, because once you put yourself out there you have like
> a big target on your back, but at least we're in the game. And we're not
> just on the sidelines throwing fiery arrows at other people and telling
> them how they're getting it wrong. We're like, "yeah, we know we're not
> perfect. But at least we're trying. And this problem, and these women
> and children perishing in the brothels, not only of India, but all around
> the world, they deserve our imperfect effort."

Those words—*imperfect effort*—hung in the air. Like most things Keith says, they are hard to argue with. It would seem that all of us are capable of making an imperfect effort. The notion of imperfection lowers the bar for participation. Yet, as twentieth century rhetorician Kenneth Burke describes, humans are "rotten with perfection."[4] His point is that our desire to know the world ("scientistically," as he says) inhibits our capacity to act. In his words, "the world is doubtless infinitely full of entities, relationships and developments, actual or potential, for which we do not have names, and never shall."[5] We cannot know everything before we act. Allowing ourselves to accept contingency, unknowability and—yes, imperfection—is a first step. Because, as Keith is quick to remind us, this is not someone else's problem to fix. It's ours.

Reflection

At the start of our interview, Keith asked me what this project was about. I told her I was studying the habits of peacemakers. She laughed and said she couldn't identify with that label and questioned whether I got the right person. I suggested hellraiser instead, to which she grinned and nodded her approval. For Keith, raising hell better characterizes how she attempts to promote enlightenment and disrupt standard business models, supply chains, and purchasing structures. Keith's story represents the antithesis of what we talked about in the opening chapter as akrasia (the tendency to suppress conscientiousness rather than risk the friction of public life). Keith seems to welcome friction and has no tolerance for people who choose convenience or withdrawal. In her words, "You don't get a moral pass." When she learned about water scarcity, she gave herself a reason to buy and donate a well. When she learned about women and children impacted by India's sex trade, she inserted herself once again. In both cases she doesn't set out to solve anything. Her horizon is duly limited by her spheres of influence and control.[6]

Keith reflects a characteristic central to practical wisdom—the acknowledgement of the essentially tragic structure of existence and a compulsion to act anyway. Or, as she puts it, "the world is screwed up," but "it isn't someone else's problem to fix." Through her story, we see practical wisdom as a recursive process that begins with some sort of awakening and continues with iterative and incremental development (teaching herself to sew a simple pattern, doing preliminary market research, forging connections with stakeholders in India, pitching her idea to them, negotiating a partnership, and generating equity within the company). At every turn, Keith seems prepared to fail ("Now, they could have said a flat 'No, thanks, not interested. We don't need your American idea, scram,' you know, and then I would have been like 'Okay fair enough'").

A willingness to accept failure is a classic risk management strategy in the business world. Headlines in publications like *Forbes Magazine* frequently ask questions of readers, such as, "Are you failing enough?" Keith's experience working in corporate America trained her to embrace this entrepreneurial attitude, this failing forward mentality. Recall the slogan she used for her company's big move—"India or Bust." You might also have noticed her tendency toward corporate speak when she uses words, such as checklists, inputs, innovation and workarounds. She also adopts sports metaphors, a favorite figure of speech among the business minded. She talked of early wins, and being in the game as opposed to just on the sidelines. Although her language and disposition reflect her background in business, her ethics and moral compass do not.

She may run her ideas through a mental rubric using strategies of cost-benefit analysis, but she differs from business analytics because she never confuses worth and value. Typically, when business minds apply cost-benefit analysis, they confuse or deliberately obfuscate the difference between worth and value. Keith, however, keeps it pretty clear—bodies are not commodities. So, even as she reflects the temperament of a cutthroat entrepreneur and adopts the language of the dog-eat-dog business world, Keith does not abide by their ethics (As she says, "There's nothing more beautiful than freedom and dignity, which is what every human being should have access to."). Keith embodies a unique combination of business ethos without business telos. Instead of pursuing the accumulation of capital (business's telos), Keith's aim is human and planetary flourishing (phronesis's telos).

Kairos, or right timing, also played a role in Keith's trajectory. Donating the well positioned her in the right place at the right time to learn about India's sex trade. She describes having had an epiphany on the way home, "Women's Pajamas!" Similar to Shawn Lent's experience of a flashbulb moment following the *Nutcracker* recital (chapter 1), Keith felt that her idea came out of nowhere. Yet, moments of unwilled reception are not all there is to it; You need to follow through on sensations.[7] Keith's immediate response, for instance, was, "Let's see if this works." Choosing to act on moral instincts is something we discussed in the previous chapter. Action from practical wisdom arises from a careful blend of intellect and intuition. American poet Lucille Clifton describes the act of writing poems in this way—"If you get too much intuition, you have sentimentality, which is not good, and with too much intellect, [you get] a whole lot of stuff that nobody knows nor cares." Instead, Clifton instructs, "It has to come from a whole human, so involve all of yourself."[8]

Drew Matott, who you meet in the next chapter, involves all of himself. Like Keith he is a risk taker, although I am not sure he would describe himself that way. Thinking in terms of risk or cost-benefit analysis presumes there are other viable options. For Matott, there are no alternatives to what he does. His mode of intervention comes from a very personal place. His story foregrounds the role of embodiment and tacit knowledge.

SEVEN

Create Space

I say "yes" to everything. And that really is
very valuable for me as a skill, to feel confident
that it's going to work out.

—DREW MATOTT

The hotel in Hamburg had a free continental breakfast so I grabbed an
extra coffee and breakfast bun to offer Drew Matott. I waited for him at a
small cafe table outside, sipping my own coffee and fiddling with my audio
recorder. I could hear the birds singing their morning song and I thought
about how birds in other countries, like people, sound both familiar and
strange. After three days in Germany, I looked forward to hearing Matott's
familiar American inflection; He was born and raised in upstate New York
and has been living as a papermaker in Hamburg for the last five years.

Matott arrived about five minutes after I sat down. He rolled up his
bicycle beside the table, and explained his tardiness was due to Schanzenstraße's morning bicycle rush hour. I knew what that meant. Cycling is
the primary mode of transportation in Hamburg. City sidewalks designate
bicycle lanes, also known as Veloroutes, with painted lines. One morning I
accidentally stepped into the bicycle lane and almost collided with a startled
cyclist. During rush hours, the Veloroutes are a blur of spinning wheels and
pedals.

Matott smiled when he saw the breakfast bun and gratefully sipped
his coffee. He leaned his bike against a nearby wall and took a seat across
from me. He didn't wear a helmet or carry a bike lock. His bike, he told me,
didn't even have brakes. He found it deserted in an alleyway a few months
back and had been meaning to fix it. He showed me how he wore out the
inner toes of his boots by using them as brakes and dragging them along the
sidewalk.

We were supposed to do our interview the day before, but Matott put it off. Instead, he invited me to his studio to see what he was working on and to meet some of his artist friends. Matott is shy and I could tell that even now he didn't look forward to the interview, but I was leaving the next day, so it was now or never. I noticed that he sat in a way that made him look like he felt cold despite the warm July weather. He held his coffee mug with two hands, curled in on himself, his knees and elbows tucked close to his body. There was an immediate sweetness to him. He didn't spread himself out like I've seen other men do. Instead, he left plenty of space for both of us.

In a way, Matott specializes in creating space for others. He moved to Hamburg from the United States a few years ago to set up a permanent papermaking studio, and a central hub for his international travel to places such as other parts of Germany, India, France, Turkey, Spain, Kosovo, Ukraine, and Poland where he teaches the ancient art of papermaking as a form of therapy, advocacy, and community building. I had never met a papermaker before Matott. I knew little about the process and even less about how it could be used to build community or heal emotional wounds. What I learned from Matott is that paper is essentially a mat of cellulose fibers that have been beaten to a pulp and collected on a screen to dry. The first paper was made from cotton rags, but later plant materials were used, such as bark, hemp, and bamboo.[1]

Papermaking began during the Han dynasty in China, around 100 BCE, and Europeans adopted the practice around the twelfth century. In the beginning, the cellulose fibers were manually pulped with a heavy wooden pestle in a stone mortar. Eventually the process was mechanized by using human-, water-, or animal-powered mills. By the time Matott encountered papermaking as an art major at Buffalo State College, he used a machine developed by the Dutch in 1680 called a Hollander beater to carry out the pulping process. The design of the Hollander beater looks a lot like a water wheel. The blades of the wheel churn over a raceway below where cellulose fibers float in water and cycle through over and over until the mixture is finely pulped into what papermakers call slurry. During the tour of his workshop, Matott gave me a pair of earmuffs to drown out the high decibel whir of the Hollander's engine. He was pulping "Make America Great Again" T-shirts, the nationalistic slogan of the Trump Administration. The pulp made beautiful red paper that could be used to write letters, send cards, or even burn in effigy. Matott gave me some sheets to take home. A friend helped me fold them into peace cranes, which now hang in my kids' playroom. A transformative process, indeed.

Matott did not initially appreciate the transformative art of papermaking, however. In fact, he actively tried to avoid it. It wasn't until his final year at Buffalo State College when his academic advisor warned him that he needed to complete The Art of Papermaking class to graduate with an art degree. "I was very resistant to it," Matott remembered, "They said it's a mandatory class for this printmaking major, which I was in, 'you have to go take [the] papermaking [class],' and I was like, 'How long can I avoid this?'" Matott's impression was that papermaking was like a hobby craft. "I thought of old ladies knitting," he said. And, at the time, Matott preferred the avant-garde. He took pride in the enormous prints he produced that involved physical strength and improvisation. "I was hitting things with chisels and like smashing things and going out on the highway and grabbing found wood objects that had been beat up and distressed and was inking them up and printing them on commercial papers," he said. Matott never gave much thought to the paper on which he printed. It was just a backdrop. He never considered how it was made or where it came from. If he needed a new sheet, he bought one from the store. But papermaking, he would learn, is not for old ladies. It is a highly physical process; one that would change his life.

MATOTT ENJOYED the messiness of papermaking—his boots were always covered in sloppy wet pulp. And as a twenty-year-old college kid, he liked the thrill of potential endangerment.

> We always had to have a studio partner there. Because it's so physical, [. . .] you weren't allowed to be in the studio by yourself. You might injure yourself—the Hollander's there, you might pull out your back moving these heavy felts and sheets. And so, you always had to have a buddy and I liked that.

The experience contrasted starkly with the time he spent in the print studio. There, he describes everything as so independent it almost felt secretive. "You kept everything so close and secret and you shared it with a few of your partnering friends, everything was so guarded," he said. By contrast, he described the paper studio as welcoming and collaborative:

> In the paper studio everything was so open, and you could talk to somebody about what they're working with and they're like, "Yeah, I'm pulping these pajamas." And people would show up with a bottle of wine or

make coffee and you know, depending on the time of day and [. . .] it was really [a family] style experience.

Matott flourishes in a family-style setting. He grew up in a big one, himself. He had five brothers and one sister. "You know, a small Catholic family," he smiled. Matott fell in the middle of his sibling lineup. His mother was a librarian. His father died in a car wreck when Matott was just five years old. "We helped raise each other," he said. The banter and rapport that he found in the papermaking studio felt a lot like his big family.

Long after his mandatory class, he found himself returning to the papermaking studio just for the company and to help with chores. There was always plenty to do like helping other artists unload the Hollander, or cleaning up after them as they moved forward with their project, or loading paper into the dry box. He also liked learning and teaching new techniques. Matott credits his proclivity for collaboration and interdependence to his mother and the way she managed the young family's tragedy.

> She did a really good job of getting us to understand that we need to get along to make things happen, to work together, to take care of each other. And she wasn't always around because she was working full-time, and so, as a large family, we came together to protect and care for and provide for each other.

Just before our interview in 2019, Matott had gone back to see family in upstate New York. An electrical fire had burned his childhood home to the ground. His brother, Kip, also an artist, was inside at the time, was badly injured as a result, and taken to the hospital.

> I went home to help receive him because he had been released from the hospital and he was doing really well. And we were kind of going through his old art. And, originally, I was going through the house trying to save his paintings and his linoleum block prints and some of the sketch books and what things I could to give him some sort of sense of comfort as he transitioned out of the hospital and into recovery mode in the real world. And he, unfortunately, one morning had pains in his chest and shortness of breath. We rushed him to the hospital, but he had a heart attack and they couldn't bring him back. And so, when I was home, not only was I there with my family to kind of help deal with the house and the return of my brother. We ended up having to deal with death, and that was really, really hard.

Matott's late father, an architect who had studied under the well-known architect Buckminster Fuller—made his living traveling all over the United States building geodesic domes, tiny houses, and different kinds of visionary structures. His father's profession instilled in Matott an appreciation for the significance of place. Although the house lost to the fire wasn't one of his father's designs, it held deep meaning for Matott. It was home to some of his favorite memories.

> Before I left, I went back through the old burned house with a hardhat and a flat shovel and kind of pawed through the ashes and pulled some pieces out that I didn't know what I was going to do with. So, I threw it all in plastic bags and into my suitcase and I flew it over here [to Hamburg]. And I wanted to have something to work with at some point, to kind of process this stuff on my own. Or for my family because they are coming to deconstruct the house.

Back in Hamburg, Matott allowed himself to unzip the suitcase. He was immediately subsumed by the heavy smell of wet decaying sheetrock and charred wood and insulation. His fingers shook as he began pulling things out and laying them on a table; mostly burned photographs and scraps of clothing. "I don't know whose clothing it was from the family. Maybe it was my sister's, maybe it was my brother's, maybe it was my past deceased brother's." (Kip was the second of Matott's brothers to die. The first was Tony, a poet.)

> I had to wash the material by hand to get rid of all the bits of nastiness that was embedded in it—like the dirt and the ash and all that—and then I hung it to dry. It was easier to identify whose clothing was what, you know, if it was a female shirt, it was my sister's or my mom's.

Seeing his family's clothes hanging on a clothesline in his papermaking studio made him think of his childhood. With seven children, his mother did laundry constantly. Instead of sorting it by person, she sorted it by item type. Pants, underwear, shirts, and socks, each in their own basket. Matott recalled his daily routine:

> Wake up in the morning, you take a bath or a shower, and you'd run to the laundry basket and you find a pair of pants that would fit you and you find a shirt that fits you and you put it on. Sometimes there wasn't anything that fit so you wore something a little bit too small or

something that's a little bit too big. So, we shared our clothing, you know. You'd be at school and you'd see your brother wearing a shirt that you like to wear.

Even the way Matott spoke about his clothes conveyed his lack of ego and sense of entitlement. His brother wore a shirt he liked to wear, not a shirt that was *his.* It was a household economy without exclusive ownership. The shirt belonged to everybody.

DURING MY TOUR of his workspace in 2019, I saw some of those clothes hanging on a line in Matott's studio. Some of them were waiting to become paper. Making paper from old clothes and other textiles begins by cutting them up into postage stamp sized squares to feed into the Hollander beater. Matott usually uses a combination of scissors and a pizza cutter. Scissors to remove buttons, pockets, and zippers. A pizza cutter to cut long strips in the cloth.

> Once you start cutting it, you can't go back, can no longer wear it. And my association with the materials started to transform immediately from clothing that I found in the burned ashes to cut up material that then goes in the Hollander, and after it comes out of the Hollander, it's clean beautiful pulp.

Matott processed something like 16 loads of material from the stuff he brought back from New York. As pulp, it was striking—a kaleidoscope of blue, gray, pink and brown. He kept some rescued photos and pieces of charred wood to lay into the wet sheets of paper as they dried. He wanted a reminder of the accident and the loss. After he finished a few pieces, he stared at the paper as it dried. The contrast was striking. "The paper was almost too beautiful," he said.

> I wanted to throw the stuff from the clothing that I'd washed off back in it, so you'd have more of the sense of the accident, I guess, the trauma that we all experienced. But at the same time, it's kind of a little bit like an airing out [. . .] it's not all dark and decay, there is some beauty in it.

It was hard to know whether Matott was talking about paper or about life when he said "it's not all dark and decay, there is some beauty in it." What came to mind were the lines from a Rilke poem, "Let everything happen to you: beauty and terror. Just keep going. No feeling is final."[2] The art of papermaking, as Matott practices it, is purifying. He loaded the Hollander with clothes holding his family's story of grief and suffering. What came out the other side was a different story—Matott and his brothers racing to the laundry basket for a clean shirt that fit. Both are true. Both happened. But now Matott could see them more clearly. He had more control over the potency of his pain.

THE REASON MATOTT filled his suitcase with remnants of the family home was because he knew that fabric holds story. He learned that while making paper in college. "That first semester [of the papermaking class] I went home on [Thanksgiving] break and I had my paper goggles on," Matott said. When he began making paper using the ancient technique, he said he started to look at all types of fabric as potential paper, wondering how it would look as pulp. What color would it make? How would the texture feel? Sometimes he would take off the shirt he wore to the studio that day and pulp it out of sheer curiosity.

During his Thanksgiving break with his paper goggles on, Matott pulled out some of his father's old writings and drawings and photographs. It was a regular habit for him. He discovered the box of his father's things when he was a teenager. Spending time with it felt like spending time with his dad.

> I pulled the box down, and I put it down next to his old typewriter and started kind of going through it again. And I remember some of the material like, you know handwritten or typed on construction paper and things like that. So, I was looking at the paper and I got to the bottom of the box and there was an old pair of his blue jeans that were paint-crusted and full of holes and a sweatshirt and a T-shirt and a handkerchief. And as soon as I touched the material, I thought, "Oh my, what would this be like to transform it into paper?"

He asked his mother if he could take the stuff back to school and turn it into paper. She hesitated. It was all she had left of her husband. During the week Matott was home, his mother visited the box. Before Matott left for school she said, "What if you transformed his clothing into paper and then printed some of his photographs and his poems onto the paper?" It was a brilliant idea.

Before he returned to school, Matott sat around the dining room table with his mother, brothers, and sister, cutting up his dad's blue jeans, removing buttons and zippers and checking pockets. As they cut, Matott and his brothers talked about what it was like to grow up without a father. It was something they never talked about before.

> We probably acknowledged, but we've never really directly talked about it. And what kind of came out through that conversation was how much we looked to different male figures in our lives, our high school teachers or coaches [. . .] We talked about how we never celebrated Father's Day, something that I've never celebrated. And then my mom got to tell us stories about how she met my father [. . .] and what it was like to be married to him—the good times and the bad times, you know. [. . .] What it really was like. And so, in many ways we came together as a family to celebrate each other and support each other in memory of my father. And that was really neat. It was really kind of wild. And I took the material with me back to Buffalo and my studio and I pulped it all up and I took the whole box with me. And while I was pulping, in my apartment I laid out all the writings and stuff and I was like, "What am I going to do with all this now?" And I realized that I didn't want to select just a few things. I wanted everything in the box to be on paper.

Matott spent the rest of the semester binding the paper into a book. Twelve books, actually. For his mother, his siblings, and his father's siblings.

He wanted the book to contain his father. He wove original writings and sketches throughout each of the twelve copies, making it difficult to tell which pieces were original and which were replicas. At the end of the school year, Matott went home and distributed the books. His family members were grateful. They each had a piece of the box from the attic. But it was giving one of the books to his uncle that changed the course of Matott's life.

> I gave it to my uncle who's closest to my father in age; they grew up together, you know, playing sports and fishing, doing everything together. But during the Vietnam War my uncle enlisted in the service because he felt like it was his duty to protect America from the Communist threat. And my father felt like it was his duty to protect America and join the anti-war movement. And, so, ever since that time their relationship was completely stressed. I didn't know this, I was unaware of this. I knew that my uncle had served in Vietnam, but I didn't know to the extent of it—of the relationship with my father. And, so, when I brought the book to him—he's also a builder and an architect and so he was in his office—and I handed him the book and he opened it up and the end pages of the book are these marbled photographs of my father's passport

photo [. . .] so he opened it up and he saw the photographs of my father, and he immediately closed it and he put it [down]. He had the
book on the table and he just started to cry. My uncle is this like, you
know, hard, hardened like kind of Vietnam vet, and I was really taken
back and he kind of pushed the book a little bit away and he had his
hand on the book and then he just started talking to me and telling
stories about my father like growing up and fishing and what it was like
and how close they were and how much this means to him. And then
he told me about their break, the severance of the relationship, and he's
like "I never—we never were able to make up after that and then he
was killed."

Matott was not prepared for the rawness of his uncle's pain. He sat with
him, witnessing his suffering. The book conjured the incompleteness of the
relationship his uncle had with his father, and the guilt he felt for not recon-
ciling while he had the chance. Matott made a point to visit his uncle more
often. Every time he did, his uncle opened a page in the book and read a
random passage or part of a letter, or traced his finger around a photograph
and told a story, bringing his brother momentarily back to life.

> That experience right there with my uncle really made me realize that
> papermaking and these processes that I was experiencing had the ability
> to have more of an impact, like a profound impact [. . .] more of an
> impact than just printing up on some paper and putting it on a gallery
> wall and having people shuffle by and, you know, have some kind of
> small experience. It could have a profound experience in somebody's
> life.

After he finished his undergraduate studies at Buffalo State, Matott
moved to Burlington, Vermont, to open a paper making mill. He and his
partner, Lydia, shopped around the city for spaces they could afford but their
budget of $400 a month limited their options. They began looking at bigger
spaces with the idea of subdividing and sharing costs with other artists and
makers. They found just what they needed—a subterranean workspace with
an open floorplan on the south end of Burlington. "I drew up some basic
plans on a napkin like where the walls will go and what the structure will be
like and then I did the numbers of how much it was going to cost and I was
like, 'Oh shit, this is a lot of money.'" Matott and Lydia set up a meeting with
the community economic development office in Burlington to get some free
financial advice. After several meetings, they had a rough business plan.

We didn't have any grants, or we didn't have any financial backers. And, so, we just had our Citi card, and I think an $18,000 limit. And, so, we went to Home Depot and [whoosh noise] $18,000 in, we started building. And we did all the plumbing and all the wiring. We maxed out our credit card and we had this strategy to rent the spaces and pay the interest plus the little bit on the credit card every month.

Matott built six private and semi-private workspaces and a gallery in the middle. He built a dark room and a paper mill. He called it Green Door Studio. Then he put an ad in the paper soliciting artists to come share the space. It worked. The subterranean studio was at full occupancy every month. Matott and Lydia paid off their Citi card in two years. Most of the artists who came had completed their undergraduate degrees and were looking for a space to work on their portfolios.

They were in the 20-to-30 age range and that [. . .] created a really dynamic and fun environment. So, it was on fire the whole time. People were coming and going and there's always somebody in the studio. We had an in-house brewer, so a guy that made us our own beer.

The atmosphere resembled the papermaking studio at Buffalo State. People showed up to take care of themselves and each other.

That's kind of when I realized that this community engagement piece was a form of art and architecture, bringing people together in a space, redefining the space and creating a culture and nourishing that culture so that you're helping people be who they want to be and be happy about who they are.

Papermaking brought people to the studio; the culture is why they stayed. Although it wasn't a geodesic dome, Matott's description suggests a certain roundness.

During the five years Matott lived in Burlington and ran Green Door Studio, he hosted free monthly public workshops. He posted flyers around the city inviting people to come make paper and asked them to bring fabric of personal significance.

I was just doing it casually as a way to, in many ways, to fuel my desire to pursue papermaking with personal clothing and with the community. But also, it was a way to kind of allow people a safe, comfortable space to tell their story as a community and maybe they would want to come back to make more paper.

And they did. Matott's workshops were very popular. Dozens attended every offering. Matott got to meet new people, hear all kinds of stories, and experiment with different kinds of fabric.

In 2004, an Iraq War veteran, also named Drew, came to one of the open workshops. He had already been exposed to papermaking and understood the basic tenets of the process. The two Drews became fast friends. "We'd have a six-pack of beer and we'd explore bookbinding or working with different fibers, and we would just kind of shoot the shit and make paper together." Matott enjoyed having a buddy in the studio, just like in his college days.

> I'll never forget one day he brought down all of his photographs and ephemera that he had brought back from his time in the service, when he was in Iraq. So, the Iraqi currency and this kind of stuff [. . .] And, so, when he brought this material down, he started showing me photographs of things [. . .] and he kind of talked about the different missions he was on and kind of sharing his story [. . .] And eventually he brought down his military uniform that he had most recently worn while he was in the service and it was still unwashed and he said, "I would like to transform this into paper."

Matott's first thought was that the durable, flame-resistant fabric would destroy his Hollander. But after seeing how the other Drew had already taken the initiative of cutting it up, removing buttons, and pulling sand and cigarette butts out of the pockets, he knew it was important and worth the risk to his Hollander.

> He made about 300 sheets of paper with that desert camouflage uniform, which is the tannish one. And he started writing letters and making journals for people he served with. He wrote to all those friends that he served with. Some of them were being incarcerated because they refused to go back to the front line.

The next thing Matott knew, he had veterans showing up at the studio with their sea bags full of uniforms saying that they wanted to make paper. The Burlington community responded with open arms. As Iraq and Afghanistan veterans arrived in the city, residents opened their homes for them to stay while they processed their uniforms. The need among this demographic was clear.

In 2006, Matott began applying for grants to fund a veteran-specific workshop at a community center. All three of the grants he applied for that year were denied. One of them came back with a handwritten note chiding him for having the gall to cut up military uniforms at a time when the nation should be supporting its men and women in battle. Matott felt like they just didn't get it. This was a form of support.

> I was like, well if we can't get funding from these organizations then, phooey to them. Let's just do it on our own. And, so, I reached out to university special collections libraries and said, "Hey, we're making paper out of military uniforms. Would you be interested in purchasing some of this work?" And they were like, "Yeah, definitely." So, then I was like, okay, if I can pull a workshop off or if we create a body of work that Veterans would be willing to donate—just one or two sheets of paper out of the hundred or so that they make—we can create a little portfolio. And so, I pitched this idea to Saint Lawrence University in Canton, New York, which is near where I grew up.

Saint Lawrence gave Matott $3,000 and the studio space to host a workshop. He used the money to pay for the veterans' travel and housed them among Canton community members like he had done in Burlington. "We spent that Veteran's Day weekend coming together and cutting up the uniforms . . . we had about 18 Veteran participants who kind of went through this process together." They created a portfolio of work and called it The Combat Paper Project. It sold eight sets immediately, which gave Matott an operating budget to continue. From there he just started knocking on doors at different universities asking if they'd like to host a papermaking workshop and telling them it would cost $3,000.

On Veterans Day 2007, Matott officially launched The Combat Paper Project. He gave lectures and demonstrations and sometimes people would approach him afterward with a check. Sometimes universities would pay extra honoraria. All the money was running through his personal checking account; it was a lot to manage. By 2010, Combat Paper had an operating budget of $116,000 through mostly donations. He received letters in the mail with checks attached from ordinary citizens saying, "Please keep doing this. This is really important to us, to see that there's something that's bringing the veterans some sort of sense of peace as they come home." But the pain of war was taking a toll on Matott. It was difficult for him to keep showing up and bearing witness to others' war stories with his whole heart.

The emotional rigor of witnessing war began to disorient Matott. He could feel himself getting lost. Ultimately, three years after its official launch, Matott decided to step away from the project. "It was very difficult being an artist," recalled Matott because, "It's great having created something so successful, but it's really, really hard to step off of a really fast-moving train, especially when I was pulling all the gears. [. . .] That was a really difficult and hard time."

When Matott announced to some of the veterans who had taken leadership roles in the organization that he wanted to do something else, they were understanding. Matott had been receiving e-mail inquiries from different therapy groups asking if he could work with children or refugees or victims of sexual assault. He liked that idea but didn't know how to begin or if he had the emotional bandwidth for it. To clear his head, he traveled for nine months—Europe, India, and Dubai. During that time "being lost and out and about," as he called it, Matott considered how he could "open it up and bring a sense of peace and reconciliation to individuals who are survivors in general." When he returned from his sojourn, he began working with an art therapist to develop what he does now—The Peace Paper Project. Peace Paper felt more genuine to who he was; the emphasis being on *peace,* rather than combat.

Eventually, the art therapy community became aware of Matott's workshops. So did the peace and justice communities. He no longer had to make cold calls asking for opportunities and support. These days, Matott keeps his schedule booked a year in advance, traveling the globe to build communal spaces just like his dad used to do. It has never been about making money for Matott.

> I want people to email me and say "Hey, we don't have any money. Will you come work with prisoners in Minneapolis?" If you don't have funds, we can find funding from the community or I can look around and see if we can find a donor or somebody. So, I say yes to everything. And that really is very valuable for me as a skill, to feel confident that it's going to work out. And I think it's really important to provide these services to the individuals who want them. Because as soon as I say no, I'm afraid that all the doors will close, and I want people to be affected by paper and to use papermaking to help their lives become better.

Having experienced it himself and having led hundreds of workshops for others, Matott knows how powerful and transformative the papermaking process can be. It is difficult and it is emotionally taxing, but he has learned to trust the process.

PEOPLE TYPICALLY ARRIVE at his workshops with a piece of clothing that holds significant trauma for them. A widower brings his wife's nightgown. A woman brings a dress in which she was assaulted. A mother brings the cardigan she wore to her son's funeral. As Matott explained:

> The material reminds them of—it puts them in a dark spot. They've held on to it because they didn't want to get rid of it. And then you know, everybody kind of shares in that. They have these wounds and this material is symbolic of their wounds. The most difficult part I found—and it's common across the board—is the cutting up of that material.

Matott begins his workshops with a quick demonstration. He brings a T-shirt, one that has some sort of story, nothing particularly dark and painful, just an anecdote about traveling or the last time he wore it. Holding scissors in one hand and the T-shirt in the other, he tells a short story about the shirt and then demonstrates how to cut it into small squares.

> I make it look so easy so everybody grabs some scissors and then they'll put 'em down, you know, and they'll lay their clothing out, often picking at the buttons, going through what's in the pockets, kind of remembering and then somebody will start cutting. And then you start to hear more people cutting and, at all the workshops, *this moment*! When people bring stuff in, everybody's really tight, you know? They're holding things really close and then they have to share a little bit of a story. Some people aren't really comfortable with that. They tell a little bit like, "this is my clothing, I had some bad experiences in it." Or some people get really into it—the day of, what their memory was— and as the cutting starts happening, you hear people start talking to their neighbor. Things loosen up a little bit.

Sometimes people bring a backup article of clothing just in case they can't bring themselves to cut up the emotionally charged one. A widower isn't ready to cut up his wife's nightgown, but he brought a pair of his son's socks so he cuts those up instead.

> My favorite part is when, after they see everybody else cutting it up, it's almost like peer pressure in some ways, "okay I can I see this now. I want to cut this up." And there's no [. . .] pressure to cut up anything. You can find your own path with this material if you're uncomfortable at all, but I think that through generating this comfortable space where people make their own decisions and their own choices, they're

reclaiming their experience, they're controlling it. And, so, you're allowing them to take control of that event and transform it.

Each person's material is loaded into the Hollander separately. While the Hollander grinds away, they stand there watching as their piece of clothing is de-threaded and broken down further, eventually turning into a wet pulpy slurry. Matott gives them earmuffs to protect their ears from the motor's grind. They stand beside the beater, combing their hand through the soft pulp as it churns in the waterway below.

> Then we drain it into buckets, and everybody first makes paper from their own material. And that's important so that they feel a direct connection with the fiber and their experience, making sure that it's really personal. But after like 10 or 15 sheets of paper, they'll start to look around at the other people's pulps for different colors. [laughs]

Matott explained that by the end of the first day, the participants become bored with their own pulp. The piece of clothing they brought to the workshop has lost some of its power, some of its potency, and they begin looking at their neighbors' bucket of pulp. "Somebody will ask somebody 'Can I pull your pink sheets? This is a beautiful color,'" said Matott. The pulp, the very fabric they gripped so tightly, was now something they were playing with and letting others play with.

> I love [. . .] I've never had anybody [. . .] How do I say this? Everybody's always wanted to share their fiber. So, it becomes community fiber and all their experiences, all that hurt and that pain no matter what the experiences were, has really transformed into a community celebration, and everybody's smiling and we turn the music up, so we're playing like Cyndi Lauper and dancing around and it's just night and day from the moment, the time that they came in, holding the fiber so close and then kind of working with it, releasing it, and then sharing it and building a sense of community and support through it.

When the paper is pressed and dried, workshop participants write on it, print photos on it, or bind it into books. They bring it home to keep, share, or send away.

Matott's faith in papermaking as a purification process has led him to expand his scope beyond offering workshops. He wants everyone to be able to transform their pain into paper. Everyone, however, does not have access to a Hollander beater. In fact, only three people in the entire world make Hollanders commercially and they are all over the age of 65. Lately, Matott has turned his attention to helping communities design and build their own Hollanders.

During our interview Matott talked about his plans for an upcoming trip to Rwanda and Sierra Leone to work with host organizations to melt down machetes and weld them together to make a Hollander beater. "They're actually collecting machetes from the killings and the maimings, and I'm going to go there and we're actually going to build the Hollander out of these old weapons of war," he explained. Instead of leading the workshops himself, Matott planned to help with the build and then teach a training workshop so leaders from the host organizations could run them. He wanted them to have sustainable access to papermaking. Quite literally, he wanted swords to become plowshares. "These countries and their situations, [are] so full of colonialism and conflict, you know, I was like, 'man . . . the last thing these countries need is an American coming in and telling them what to do and how to do it.'"

The pandemic, of course, put the kibosh on Matott's travel plans. Still, he refused to waylay his democratic ideal, so he used his time in quarantine to publish a free online guidebook with do-it-yourself instructions on how to build a Hollander. He offered virtual support as much as he could and when travel bans were lifted, some organizations made trips to his studio in Hamburg for troubleshooting tips and tricks.

MATOTT LOVES what he does. He is an amateur in the true sense of the word— motivated by love. It is rare to meet people like him. I asked how I could advise my college students, who come to my office worried about choosing the right major, and who end up on paths that don't align with their interests because they're afraid. He said, "What a painful thing to go through life and just not like to go to work and be in these situations where you're not happy." He continued:

> I think that it's risky in today's society and in American culture because we are taught to take the path where you know what's going to happen and make these decisions and x, y, z and things add up. But if you follow your heart, these things come together. I think the other bit is to not be afraid of taking risks. Go towards the things that give you butterflies in your stomach, the things that make you nervous, that you shy away from. Continue to be challenged and to challenge yourself. And I

think the more that you go towards things that make you feel nervous and afraid, the more comfortable you get with yourself and your environment, and the more that you find yourself making decisions that are honest to you.

Matott's relationship to comfort is unusual. Generally speaking, the rest of us spend much of our lives seeking comfort and trying to avoid discomfort, but Matott lives in such a way that he never allows himself to become too comfortable. He moved to Germany in 2016 without knowing one word of the language. In 2021, the German government recognized him as one of the country's fine artists, awarding him 10,000 Euros and a full healthcare, disability, and pension package. So now he enjoys some security, but security is not the same as comfort.

Matott continues to push himself. He travels to new places and invites strangers to talk about their most painful memories. He rides a bike with no brakes. And, to my amazement, he sat through our entire hour-long interview without taking a single bite of his breakfast bun. When we finally finished and I unclipped the microphone from his shirt, he stood for a hug. Then he put the bun between his teeth, grabbed his bike by the handlebars, swung a leg over the side and pedaled off. Rush hour in Schanzenstraße was over. He was heading back to his studio to transform his family's painful house fire into beautiful paper.

Reflection

I considered titling this chapter "Create Pasture," but worried it would be too confusing. Pasture is a word I use to connote mental, physical, and spiritual spaciousness. The first time I used pasture in this way was to describe a romantic relationship that I admired. In my effort to express the quality I observed, I said, "They seem to give each other a lot of pasture." What I meant was that both partners exhibited a fundamental respect for the dignity and autonomy of the other. Since then, I have found the word pasture to be supremely useful in allowing me to conceptualize relational dynamics in a new way, including the relationship we have with ourselves. American culture, devout in bootstrap mythology, conditioned me to keep my nose to the grindstone, so to speak. I hadn't realized until relatively recently the value of personal pasture. Now I understand—You need to give yourself space to become who you are.

Matott's story is about creating space for himself and for other people. His workshops are, as he put it, "a form of art and architecture, bringing people together in a space, redefining the space and creating a culture and nourishing that culture so that you're helping people be who they want to be and be happy about who they are." The space, as he explains, is both physical and metaphorical. Most of the time, Matott has limited control over the physical space because he travels wherever he is invited. So, the spaciousness he cultivates has more to do with the atmosphere—the spirit, mood, or tone in which he conducts his workshops ("I always tell people, 'there's no pressure to cut up anything.'"). He supports the autonomy of the participants. He respects their limitations and celebrates their milestones. In other words, his workshops are like wide open pastures.[3]

Sometimes spaciousness can feel unsettling. In the introductory chapter, I discussed the idea of drift, the feeling of groundlessness that arises from contemporary conditions of fragmentation, dislocation, and disconnection. I wrote how these conditions are created and sustained at the structural level, but that I hope we might become inspired to act out of this discomfort, to respond with phronesis rather than akrasia. Matott is someone who has taught himself to exert agency amid uncertainty. He makes a point to move toward things that give him "butterflies in [his] stomach," the "things that make [him] nervous" because he sees those as opportunities for personal growth and expansion. Pushing against those boundaries is how he creates more pasture for himself.

It takes reflection and self-awareness to identify personal points of resistance ("paying 'a certain kind of attention' to the self in the world," is how I wrote it in the introduction). And it takes courage to let yourself relax enough so that you can move toward those uncomfortable spaces, whether they be spiritual or material. Philosopher and medical ethicist Ann Mongoven writes about a civic virtue she calls disciplined vulnerability.[4] I like the concept because the word vulnerability communicates our inherent interdependence and the word disciplined suggests that it is a virtue that can be cultivated. Mongoven argues that humility and active listening help "foster such openness" but warns that it's also important to "develop the prudence necessary to resist its excess."[5] Matott's experience with The Combat Paper Project is an example of this dialectic tension. He was open and responsive to the needs of the veteran community and prudent enough to know when it was time for him to step back and reconcile his own interests and commitments. He described the process as difficult ("it's great having created something so successful but it's really, really hard to step off of a really fast-moving train"). The notion of disciplined vulnerability calls attention to discernment and choice. Like some of the other stories you've read so far discernment and subsequent choices serve to clarify Matott's next steps.

Clarifying the next step is not the same as envisioning an outcome. Recall that practical wisdom is a capacity for virtuous action in the face of uncertainty. Openness to uncertainty is a skill for Matott. Like any skill, he develops it through repetition. When he started Green Door Studio, "We didn't have any grants . . . we just had our Citi card." Or when he couldn't get anyone to support his idea for Combat Paper, he thought, "Phooey to them. Let's just do it on our own." Matott exhibits a quality we've seen elsewhere, a sort of wild audacity that's goaded by practical wisdom's telos to bring about well-being for all.

The next story continues this theme of embracing uncertainty and saying yes to the unknown. It also picks up on ideas related to trust, vulnerability, perspective, and smallness. The person you meet works creatively within the constraints of circumstance and figures out how to bring together the right people at the right time for the right reason to forge an uncharted path one step at a time.

EIGHT

Think Big, Step Small

Start doing something, and it starts
materializing before your eyes.

—KEITH ALANIZ

I nearly walked by the coffee shop where we were supposed to meet. The brick building on my right was so covered with graffiti and street art that I almost missed the Sawada Coffee sign marking the nondescript entrance. I was in Chicago's West Loop, a formerly industrial area, now a foodie neighborhood. Historic warehouses like the one I was about to enter have become home to some of the hippest, most creative eateries in the city. I heaved open the big metal door to find myself facing someone's backside telling me that I was last in line for coffee. I glanced around to see if someone looked like they were waiting to meet me. I was looking for a man named Keith Alaniz. I had never met him before but had an idea of what he looked like from a photo online.

The space was warm and lively. Freshly roasted coffee pervaded my senses. Edison bulbs draped from the ceiling on long sweeping strings. Large industrial windows lined the wall. Free wireless internet kept the place packed with young people whose faces were lit by the bluish glow of their laptop screens. They sat shoulder-to-shoulder around an old wooden Ping-Pong table in the center of the room. The atmosphere was fast-paced and gruff, but not unfriendly. My phone buzzed with a text message from Alaniz saying he was on his way. I felt relieved. I always prefer to be the person waiting.

As the coffee line progressed, I turned my attention to the big black menu board behind the bar. I wanted to plan my order, so I didn't panic in front of Alaniz. I saw something called a "Military Latte" which I learned was the shop's signature drink—an espresso-matcha combo that creates the brown-green look of camouflage in your cup. The baristas—mostly young, bearded, and heavily tattooed men—wore camouflage T-shirts and the bar itself was painted with American iconography like a screaming eagle emblazoned with flags. Other decor included a vintage pinball machine, a retro heavyweight boxing bag and skateboards hanging on the wall like works of art.

I saw Alaniz walk through the door, so I motioned for him to come join me in line. Despite this being our first encounter, the pace and volume of the place kept our greetings brief. Besides, he looked somewhat dazed. He and his wife had a brand-new baby at home; their second. I bought us each a signature latte drink and his wife a chocolate donut to thank her for sparing him for a few hours. As a new mother myself, I understood the sacrifice. He tucked the donut into the leather mail bag slung over his shoulder, and we took our drinks to a picnic table outside.

Sounds of the street replaced the buzz of the coffee shop. A city bus hissed and grunted to a stop a few yards away. I worried about the noise affecting my audio recorder because Alaniz spoke so softly. I asked him if he picked Sawada Coffee because of the military theme. He laughed and said he had never really noticed it before. One of the reasons Alaniz and I were meeting was to talk about his experience in the military. As for the coffee shop, "it's just a coincidence," he said.

Alaniz has soft, round, pensive eyes. He didn't look like what I imagined a hardened war veteran to look like. He began by telling me he didn't join the military to go to war. He joined to create peace. "I don't think anybody, you know people in the military, feel like they're out there to cause war," he said. "I think everybody feels like they're there to make peace; . . . that's why I would venture to guess most people join the military, not to go and fight." Alaniz graduated from Texas A&M in 2006 as a commissioned officer from the Army's ROTC program. His diploma announced a degree in engineering and bore the signature of the university's president at the time, Robert Gates. A few weeks later Alaniz received his first deployment orders, bearing the same signature. President George W. Bush had appointed the Texas A&M President to be the 22nd US Secretary of Defense.

ALANIZ WAS on his way to Iraq. The US invasion had begun three years earlier. At this point in the war, the American death toll was estimated as 3,000. Reports were surfacing about US troops facing material shortages, including body armor.[1] Mothers were sending bulletproof vests in care packages to their sons. American resources were split across two warfronts—Iraq and

Afghanistan. One Pentagon study found that as many as 80 percent of the Marines killed in Iraq by 2006 could have survived if they had regulation body armor that reached their shoulders, sides, and torso.[2] Alaniz's orders were to Baghdad, the heart of sectarian violence.

> That was my first experience with the military, like right after train-ing, going straight into very high intensity combat, which is really, it's tough to put an adjective on it, but it's quite an experience, especially [because] you're really seeing the epitome, or the nadir, of things going bad. This is the worst thing, this is like the worst possible situation, there's a total civil war, you have two ethnic and religious groups that are fighting each other, both of which are fighting the Americans, and we're all here, just like stuck in between and trying to survive and make a difference.

Alaniz deployed as a combat engineer to search for and dismantle road-side bombs. His unit's job was to walk 20 meters ahead of heavily armored patrol vehicles sweeping the ground with a metal detector searching for im-provised explosive devices (IEDs). "All you have time to think about is just your immediate—" he paused. His eyes flickered down then up again to meet mine, "quite literally the next 12 feet of road in front of you." In 2006, the year of Alaniz's deployment, the US Department of Defense created an organization devoted specifically to "defeating the IED." By 2011, 60 per-cent of American fatalities in Iraq resulted from IEDs.[3] It was the weapon that defined the war.

Alaniz's first tour in Iraq lasted thirteen months. That means for more than a year he walked twelve feet at a time, each step an odd mixture of hope and fear. Would it be better to find an IED? Or to not find one? Eleven months after returning to the states he re-deployed for a second tour in the same country. He was exhausted. "When I joined the military, I never assumed that I would be there very long, I thought I would do my initial call and then get out." His eyebrows furrowed. At the time, the de-ployment cycles to Iraq were relentless. The Bush administration eventually came under criticism for deploying US service members at unsustainable rates.[4]

After his second tour in Iraq, Alaniz was burned out. More than two years of consistent exposure to the stressors and traumas of war were taking a toll on him. For someone who didn't join the military to go to war, he sure was experiencing a lot of it. "I have distinct memories of soldiers asking . . . my thoughts on what are we *doing* here? And it's like well, how do you answer those kinds of questions? Because you know, we're just, we're just there trying to do our jobs," Keith remarked.

When rumors began to circulate about a potential deployment to Afghanistan, Alaniz started surveying his options. He did not want to deploy as a combat engineer again. He learned about an opportunity to participate in a program called AFPAK Hands—an initiative developed by General McChrystal [the Army general who led the Joint Special Operations Command (JSOC) and the International Security Assistance Force (ISAF)] to assemble a cohort of experts in Afghanistan with specialized training in language, culture, and counterinsurgency. Their mission was to establish long-term relationships with Afghan tribal leaders and government officials to foster stability and positive change. Alaniz jumped at the chance. "Especially after my experience in Iraq, I thought like 'Okay, I need to have this kind of experience in the military where we are doing something other than being 'trigger pullers' as they call it.'" Alaniz enrolled in the military's intensive language training and began studying all things Afghan. He even began reading the poetry of the thirteenth century Persian poet Rumi. He didn't know much about Rumi or poetry, but the book was a gift from a friend. "It was a cool little poetry book where I had the Farsi writing on the one side and the English translation on the other side; I was using it to study the language."

Being able to speak even just a little bit of the language was eye-opening for Alaniz. He could make congenial ice-breaking conversations with locals, and he became known as "that American who knows Dari" (Dari and Farsi are essentially two accents of the same language but Dari is distinct to Afghanistan. Farsi refers to what is spoken in Iran). Looking back, his tours in Iraq and Afghanistan were as different as night and day. Without access to the local language in Iraq, he could not understand the Iraqi people. He described himself as "operating with a blindfold," an image that captures the overall sense of chaos, confusion, and distress. But in Afghanistan, speaking the language and being able to participate, even minimally, in cultural practices gave him perspective.

> What always got me is when people would say, "Oh they're Afghans, they're just crazy" or "It's just a crazy situation, it doesn't make any sense." Like, no! It makes perfect sense, and these are perfectly rational people, we just don't understand the full context [. . .] they're making the best decisions for themselves under the circumstances. So, if we can't understand, it's our lack of knowledge not their irrationality.

Ultimately Alaniz did two tours of duty in Afghanistan, both to Badakhshan, the northeastern most province up in the mountains.

During his first deployment, he managed a construction program for the Army Corps of Engineers. He learned how to conduct business in Afghanistan. "I guess it's not very different from business here, except that, you know, there's not teams of lawyers to litigate disputes . . . a lot of times when there's disputes it comes down to people with rifles, you know, and like standoffs." In that role, he settled disagreements over broken or voided contracts. His language skills and developing cultural knowledge helped him navigate fragile and fraught business partnerships.

When I arrived [in Badakhshan] we had a bunch of broken contracts where the prime contractor, who was usually from Kabul or international, had come in and hired a bunch of locals to do work, didn't pay the locals, bailed on the contract and just left town, and so all these locals thought the US government owed them money but actually we had no ability to pay them, and there's a lot of negotiation and reworking these contracts to procure them locally. But we were able to get all these projects started again by just understanding what the local context of the situation was and why they were so mad that they were out, you know, ten, twenty thousand dollars [. . .] So that kind of showed me how our best intentions of going in there and building infrastructure had actually caused a lot of anger and strife because of our lack of understanding of what was happening on the ground.

For his second deployment to Afghanistan, Alaniz served as a government liaison for the Special Operations Community. He worked with district and provincial governors to understand community needs and identify projects that the Americans could help with in exchange for information and influence. "It's all about networking," Alaniz explained. He gave an example of building a new air conditioning unit for a government official. In response, said Alaniz, "he was like, 'Oh, here's a list of 20 Taliban people and where they're located.'" Alaniz enjoyed his work as part of the AFPAK Hands program and earned a reputation among locals as a cultural ambassador, of sorts.

One day, a local farmer called Haji Yoseph showed up in the doorway of Alaniz's makeshift plywood office. Alaniz has no idea how the farmer ended up there. Maybe he heard from other locals about "an American who speaks Dari" or maybe he came to the base and one of the soldiers pointed him to

Alaniz's office. Regardless, the farmer showed up with a business proposal for Alaniz to help him sell saffron.

> I didn't know a lot about saffron at the time, but he brought this red spice to me, he said, "I grow more of this, but I can only sell it in my local market." And you know, he's talking about his village market so he was looking for opportunities to sell outside of his village market and so I just said, "Okay. Well, let me see what I can do."

When the farmer left, Alaniz got online and started reading about saffron. He learned that saffron is the most valuable spice in the world with a rich history dating back to Cleopatra and Alexander the Great. Alaniz remembers thinking, "This could be interesting."

Haji Yoseph left samples and a CD full of pictures and marketing materials. It wasn't uncommon for locals like him to hear variations of "let me see what I can do" from American service personnel. But fortunately for Haji Yoseph, Alaniz was different. His soul-shattering experience in Iraq had changed him. He wanted to do what he joined the military to do—to create peace.

> It seems like the rational thing would be just to take care of yourself and do what's best for yourself, but if everybody was just doing what's best for themselves, we would be working in a world of diminishing good, you know? Like I mean, we'd be spiraling out of control.

Alaniz witnessed such a spiral in Iraq. He called it "the nadir of things going bad." Now in Afghanistan, he had an opportunity, coupled with a fledgling skillset, that could possibly help him do some real good.

After more than 30 years of war, Afghanistan has been cut off from the international marketplace. The country used to have a substantial market share in raisins, but war disabled that avenue. Afghan farmers, especially in remote regions like Haji Yoseph's, can barely sell goods outside of their villages.[5] On top of that, having 150,000 troops stationed in the country deeply distorted its domestic economy. As Alaniz explained, "You have the best English speakers and the best educated Afghans operating as truck drivers, driving around foreigners, and not being doctors or lawyers or businesspeople." For decades, Afghanistan has been primarily an economy of war.

> That's what's really amazing and really endearing about the Afghan people. There is this endless spring of hope, you know, even the people my

age and younger, they've only known war, but they still have this hope of a better tomorrow. And they work hard for it [. . .] they seek opportunity. I mean, it's just incredible, to live in their circumstances where lives can be lost randomly and unexpectedly, and to still have hope that's not how it's always going to be.

Alaniz became determined to work on behalf of Haji Yoseph's hope. He brainstormed ideas and dreamed up scenarios. He considered all he had learned about how to conduct business in Afghanistan. Although he couldn't picture the outcome exactly, he was certain of what he hoped for. "It doesn't have to be the clearest vision," he said, "but you should have some direction that you're headed towards, some sort of framework of where you want to be, where you want to go, then just don't be afraid to take the first steps in that direction." When I heard this, my mind flashed to Alaniz taking careful steps along a dusty road in Iraq, just twelve feet at a time.

AS WE CONTINUED sipping our coffee and listening to the throng of Chicago traffic, Alaniz told me about his most recent trip to Badakhshan Province. He visited a few months prior to our interview and said with amazement that he was starting to feel like a local. "I just walked around in business clothes and took taxis." He had been out of the military for a few years by this point, and it had been six years since his first deployment there. His memories of being a soldier in that province commingle with his new role as a businessperson and job creator. When he thinks of Afghanistan today, he does not think of war. He thinks of skyscraping mountain ranges and a purple sea of crocus flowers that you can smell before you can see. His recent trip was to oversee a cumin harvest.

> They grow this wild black cumin and it's a cumin but, there's like this family of fennel seeds, right? So, it's different from what you would buy at the store [. . .] It's very special, and so it's grown wild in the mountains of the Hindu Kush and [for] these villagers in these very isolated villages, this is one of their primary sources of income; they go around and just gather this cumin from this shrub and we've purchased like 20 percent of the production this year [. . .] That's really exciting because we're able to touch like thousands of other people on the other side of the country and in these very isolated places that really need this sort of income, and then hopefully be able to provide the US consumer with another spice from Afghanistan.

Wild black cumin is the second spice Alaniz hopes to bring to the American consumer. The first, of course, being saffron. Thinking back to his first encounter with Haji Yoseph, Alaniz smiled and said, "I don't know if he, in his wildest dreams, would have thought of selling his saffron on the shelves of US stores. I don't think he would have conceptualized that, but here we are." "Here" refers to partnerships with top American restaurants, meal-kit services like Blue Apron, and large-scale supermarkets such as Whole Foods and Kroger, all of which now carry saffron sourced directly from Afghanistan farmers like Haji Yoseph.

The initial steps toward creating what would become an international public benefit corporation began as a casual, impromptu conversation between old friends. Alaniz was still on deployment in Afghanistan. His friend, Kim Jung, also an Army Engineer who he met on an earlier deployment was in business school at Harvard. As Alaniz tells it:

> I think we were just talking on Skype one day and I was asking how business school was and she's asking me how deployment was [. . .] She was talking about how she had a class, an entrepreneurship class or something like this, and they need to come up with a business idea, and I was like "Well, I've got an idea."

Alaniz told Jung about Haji Yoseph and about saffron and the harvesting process. He told her his ideas and his hopes and together they batted possibilities back and forth about how they could help Afghan farmers gain access to Western markets.

> Kim's one of my best friends and I know if I ever have a crazy idea, Kim's the one to tell it to, because she's just as audacious as I am in pursuing things like that. So, we both got really excited about it and the possible ways of doing this.

Jung submitted a proposal for her entrepreneurship class at Harvard and as soon as the semester ended, she flew to Afghanistan to see Alaniz so they could talk logistics. It was the summer between her first and second year of business school. "Because of my mission," explained Alaniz, "I had a kind of a long leash on what I did, so I was able to go meet her in Kabul, and we met with Haji Yoseph, and, you know, in the meantime I had made relationships with other farmers that are growing saffron."

On her trip home to the states, Kim had a suitcase full of saffron. Neither she nor Alaniz knew exactly what to do with it. "We started thinking like, 'Okay, maybe a couple restaurants and a couple of farmers and we can do some good.'" The Afghan farmers also had relatively low expectations. They were skeptical of American "help."

> We paid a foreigner's price for the saffron because none of them believed we would return, but then we kept coming back year after year, and then they learned to trust us and we were able to develop a business relationship with all these farmers—and the ones we started with have done extremely well.

At the time of those initial saffron sales, Alaniz was wrapping up his second and final deployment in Afghanistan. He was getting out of the military. He and Jung brought on another Army Veteran Emily Miller, who had graduated West Point with Jung and was her best friend at business school. The three of them moved to Chicago and began developing their business ideas in earnest. They rented an old, abandoned meatpacking warehouse on the South Side called The Plant. They created a website, bought some meal prep containers, and printed labels. They called their business Rumi Spice.

> The Afghans understand who Rumi is and they have very high admiration for him as a poet and philosopher. And his philosophy is really about connecting people and the connectivity of people in the world and nature, and that's really what we were trying to bring to the consumer—an ability to connect with people on the other side of the world who you may only know as bad actors in this news cycle, where you only hear stories where the Afghans aren't real people. But this allows you to connect to these people who are producing your spices and your food, and you know, when you use that in your food, it should tell a story, and you should feel a connection with the people who produced it, even if they're on the other side of the world.

Six years later, Alaniz is still in awe of the company's progress. His attention has been so fixed on the next twelve feet ahead that he has barely given himself a chance to look behind. "It's really surprising where we're at today," he said incredulously.

> We're a brand on the shelf, and we've had a lot of great press, are really fortunate with that, and what I'm most proud of is how the Afghans have grown [. . .] we've created the opportunity and they've risen to the occasion, and they've bettered their processes and met food safety regulations and allowed us to scale to the size that we are. People always think that the Afghan part is the hardest part, but at this point that's

the easiest part. They're pretty good at what they do. The hard part is growing a business and selling in the US.

The reason saffron is so expensive is because it is difficult to grow and even more difficult to harvest. It grows in harsh, arid mountain terrain, which Alaniz described as a "moonscape." Saffron comes from the rusty-red stigma of a pale purple crocus plant. Each flower produces just three stigmas. Those three stigmas are separated by hand from the blossom and dried. One gram of saffron requires about 150 flowers. And the stigmas must be processed within days of the flowers being harvested. It is a process that typically occurs in the farmers' homes because it is traditionally considered women's work. This means the farmers have a capacity constraint on what they can produce based on how many women are in their household or in their village. To get around this constraint, Rumi Spice crowdsourced funds to open a local processing plant in Herat. Within two months of launching a Kickstarter campaign, they had $33,000 to rent a space that would employ hundreds and eventually thousands of Afghan women whose wages would be paid directly to them and not, as tradition dictates, to the male head of the household.

Initially, even though the idea made perfect business sense on paper, it proved to be a significant cultural hurdle. Before accepting employment for women who would work in the facility, the male heads of household toured the facility to ensure its safety. They also required a mandate that the women return home by dusk. Rumi Spice proved assurances and processing in Herat got underway.

> We didn't set out with the intention to impact women as part of our mission, but that's been a substantial part of our impact [. . .] giving women direct wages, you know, allowing them to work outside the home, and it changes the way they think about themselves and the way their family views them.

Alaniz told me about a woman named Hassina who began as a laborer extracting stigmas in the processing plant. Now she is chief operating officer of Rumi Spice, Afghanistan. She manages seven women who each manage hundreds of others. Hassina, who Alaniz imagines to be in her mid-20s (Afghans don't celebrate birthdays), is the oldest in a family of all daughters. The Taliban abducted her father when she was very young, so her family struggled to survive. Her mother earned money however she could— cleaning homes or doing laundry. When the opportunity presented itself,

Hassina jumped at the chance to work in the saffron industry. Now she is in a management role and her sisters look up to her, envisioning a life for themselves outside of the home. "Her sisters have big dreams and she's able to provide for their whole family," Alaniz smiled. "It's just really powerful . . . it's such a tragic story, you know, and that could have gone . . .," he trailed off. "I mean just to maintain hope in that kind of situation—it's just really inspiring, really powerful."

Afghanistan agriculture comes down to a battle between flowers. There's the poppy flower, grown for opium, and the crocus flower, grown for saffron. For Afghan farmers, if they are able, it's an easy decision to grow saffron because the income from saffron is six times greater, especially since Rumi Spice opened up the marketplace. The other reason for farmers to avoid poppy is because it's so dangerous.

> They have to work with the Taliban and it's a lot harder to work with the Taliban than with business people, [Working with the Taliban] you always have the danger of the government burning your fields down, the US burning your fields down, you have this risk and you have to take these really devious loans with the Taliban to grow and it's not a good business to be in, but they do it because of a lack of an alternative.

Rumi Spice's principal mission is to make saffron a viable economic alternative for Afghan farmers. It began with a suitcase of saffron from ten farmers, give or take. Now the company purchases crocus flowers from more than a thousand farmers. According to Alaniz, about two-thirds of the farmers he currently works with were former poppy growers. "I wish we could get everybody in the US to use saffron more often and we could, by doing that, win the war and eradicate poppies." He grinned at the romance of his idea. "If everybody just said like for the next year, I'm just gonna try to use saffron every week." We both sort of chuckled, each of us wishing for an end to the war, envisioning a federal directive to eat more paella.

When Haji Yoseph first approached Alaniz, neither of them could have anticipated what would happen. Even Alaniz admits that the idea for Rumi Spice didn't jump right out at him. He said it was the result of a series of small decisions.

> I'm kind of an analytical data guy and I'm always like, you know, you can find an optimal decision usually to your next couple of decisions, right? But you can only do that so far and then uncertainty takes over and you don't really know what's going to happen ten, fifteen steps

down the road [. . .] It was just kind of like start doing something, and it starts materializing before your eyes.

As we walked our empty mugs back inside to the coffee shop's busing station, I asked Alaniz if he had a favorite Rumi poem. He paused, and said, "As you walk the way, the way appears." He set his mug in the bin. I heard the poem echo; I pictured him in Iraq with a metal detector. I pictured him in Afghanistan talking with locals. And I pictured him traveling the Salang Pass in the mountains of the Hindu Kush looking for wild black cumin.

Reflection

Sometimes, learning what you don't want brings into clearer focus what you do want. Alaniz's deployment experiences were edifying in this way. His time in Iraq helped him see what he did not want from his military service—confusion and powerlessness. His idea for what he did want was still fuzzy, but he knew it was "something other than being [a] 'trigger puller.'" When he saw the opportunity to have a different kind of deployment experience through the AFPAK Hands program, he applied.

For two years Alaniz worked closely with his counterparts in Afghanistan, learning their language, culture, and needs. The experience elicited what rhetorical scholars call a critical interruption, a point at which we find ourselves questioning the taken-for-granted ways of doing things and feeling called to bring about change.[6] Alaniz's interruption occurred through his work with the locals and with the help of his newfound language skills and cultural awareness. He could see more clearly how willful ignorance contributed to frustration and violence ("If we can't understand, it's our lack of knowledge, not their irrationality"). Communication scholar Michael Hyde considers critical interruptions to be "the call of conscience," and a signal to initiate change. Hyde writes, "Conscience calls. We hear it as we stand in the midst of our temporal openness, anxiously struggling with the 'whence' and 'whither' of our existence, and getting ready to choose, to act, and perhaps to change our lives for the 'better.'"[7] From this perspective, we can see a connection between critical interruptions and phronesis because phronesis comprises "the insight that precedes noble action in the public sphere." As a source of insight, critical interruptions contribute to the phronetic process. Yet, action is not guaranteed by insight. As Hyde describes, a critical interruption produces an edginess, a "getting ready to act" positioning. It's a call for creativity, imagination, and invention.[8]

The capacity to imagine is connected to the capacity to act. In the introduction I discussed the importance of storytelling in this regard and how the stories we tell about our lives shape our lives. Alaniz didn't want the same old war story. He wanted something different. He wanted a new ending, even if he didn't know what that ending looked like exactly. ("It doesn't have to be the clearest vision, but you should have some direction that you're headed towards, some sort of framework of where you want to be, where you want to go, then just don't be afraid to take the first steps in that direction.") The insight he gleaned from his critical interruption had to do with zero-sum relationships. His consciousness called on him to do something different. "If everybody was just doing what's best for themselves, we would be working in a world of diminishing good," observed Alaniz. This was quite a revelation for a soldier in a war zone, where zero-sum dynamics is the name of the game.[9]

Getting clear about what doesn't work, what contributes to "a world of diminishing good," as he put it, helped Alaniz clarify what he hoped for—some sort of alternative to zero-sum dynamics.[10] When the farmer visited his office asking for help, Alaniz took it as an opportunity to take his first shaky steps toward a new ending. He said yes to the farmer even though he didn't know what that meant. And he recognized rather quickly that he didn't know the first thing about Saffron. He also understood the structural constraints of his situation. He was a soldier in a war zone and, while he enjoyed "a long leash," it was a leash, nonetheless. He knew couldn't affect change on his own and that he would need to reach out.

International peacebuilding scholar John Paul Lederach considers collaboration a key ingredient to making positive change. He describes the importance of asking what he calls the "critical yeast question"—Who within a given situation, if brought together, would have the capacity to make things grow toward a desired end?[11] For Alaniz, his go-to leavening agent had always been his best friend, Kim Jung. Not only did Jung share his audacity and spunk, but she also happened to be in an entrepreneurship class at Harvard (kairos). Together Alaniz and Jung imagined possible ways to improve marketplace access. Their dreams were big (far-reaching international trade, not to mention "win[ning] the war and eradicat[ing] poppies"), but they kept their next steps relatively small with the goal of connecting "maybe a couple of restaurants and a couple of farmers." Slowly, their network scaled up and the project grew in unimaginable ways with the mission expanding to women's employment.

When I checked in with Alaniz in late September 2021 after listening to news stories about the US's messy withdrawal from Afghanistan, he told me that Rumi Spice was still going strong and preparing for its next saffron harvest in about a week. He said the collapse of the banking system caused the biggest disruption to the company's operations, but they were able to find an independent remittance system to transfer funds. Alaniz credits the company's resilience amid US withdrawal to working within the constraints of local culture and custom or, in his words, "by following the law of the land." As of Winter 2024, Alaniz told me that "despite the Taliban takeover, we're still providing jobs for women" and "supporting about 10,000 livelihoods in Afghanistan." In addition to saffron and cumin, Rumi Spice has added dill seed, caraway, coriander, fennel and a few Middle Eastern culinary blends toward to goal of "connecting people and cultures through food."

Conclusion

Doing Peace

Oh, what'll you do now, my darling young one?

—BOB DYLAN, "A HARD RAIN'S A-GONNA FALL," 1962

Peace is a verb. It is something we do. It is not a state of ethereal tranquility that exists outside our realm of influence. We do peace and we do justice. Just like we do war, and we do violence. It is important to get clear about this because our actions define us; they reflect who we are as individuals and as a collective.

In John Steinbeck's 1941 travelog documenting a six-week expedition to collect marine specimens in the Gulf of California, he describes the process of objective observation—how scientists look into tide pools and draw conclusions about the little creatures they see based on the behavior they observe. But we don't do this with our own species, observes Steinbeck. Then he posits what conclusions could be drawn if we were to look at our own species in the same way:

> If we used the same smug observation on ourselves that we do on hermit crabs we would be forced to say, with the information at hand, "It is one diagnostic trait of *Homo sapiens* that groups of individuals are periodically infected with a feverish nervousness which causes the individual to turn on and destroy, not only his own kind, but the works of his own kind. It is not known whether this be caused by a virus, some airborne spore, or whether it be a species reaction to some meteorological stimulus as yet undetermined."

Steinbeck goes on to write that it doesn't need to be this way, but until we, as a species, exhibit "a contrasting habit pattern," then the simple conclusion

: 129 :

is that we are what we do and that what we predominantly do is violence. According to Steinbeck, it would take "twenty, thirty, fifty years without evidence of our murder trait" to modify such a conclusion but "so far there is no such situation." I am haunted by Steinbeck's analogical reasoning first because it is hard to argue with and second because he leaves room for hope by suggesting that we could change. All we need to do is show sustaining evidence of "a contrasting habit pattern."[1]

Doing peace is an example of a contrasting habit pattern because doing peace is the opposite of doing war, violence, and destruction. Doing peace means bringing about the conditions that support human and planetary flourishing. To do peace is to be creative, imaginative, and collaborative. Peace represents the best of us. It is the manifestation of human excellence. If I were to fill in the silhouette of hope implied by Steinbeck's thought experiment, the conclusions I would want drawn about our species is that we appear to be an altruistic and collaborative society, averse to violence, and preoccupied with securing the wellbeing of each other and the planet.

Peace and Practical Wisdom

Throughout this book, I've positioned phronesis at the heart of peace because phronetic action is peaceful action. Both peace and phronesis are simultaneously process and outcome; their purposes define their methods and vice versa. Peace and phronesis share a similar goal, but they are not the same thing. Peace is broader than phronesis with a more expansive horizon. Phronesis, on the other hand, anchors itself in the specificity of the immediate present. You might think of phronesis as the practical application of peace. Or, to use a war metaphor, peace is strategy and phronesis is tactic.[2] They share the same end goal (telos).

The ancient Greeks considered eudaemonia to be the telos of phronesis, which translates as "the good life," "wellbeing," "the greatest good," or "ethical excellence," depending on which scholar you read.[3] Diverse definitions aside, nearly all scholars agree that eudaemonia is grounded in the virtue of justice, which Aristotle considered "the sovereign virtue" because it is "the only virtue that is regarded as someone else's good."[4] Justice is about protecting others' pursuit of happiness. So, if we say that the telos of phronesis is about bringing the greatest good and protecting the wellbeing of others, then that sounds very much like my definition of peace (the promotion of flourishing). Because phronesis manifests on the ground level, embodied by regular people, it is more amenable to study and imitation.

The stories you've read in this book, along with my reflections on them, delineate some useful habits for enacting peace through practical wisdom. Specifically, they emphasize habits related to humility, trust, flexibility, self-questioning, integrity, courage, and hope. Each story contains these habits in different ways, by emphasizing different verbs, to give a clearer sense of what real change can look like. It begins with showing up. In the introductory chapter I made a case for the value of strangers showing up for one another. I explained how the very real structural and systemic problems we face require that we look beyond the self and risk engaging with others; not to solve those problems, but to ameliorate their harmful symptoms and make life just a little bit more livable. The people you've read about exhibit some characteristics essential to showing up and embodying intersectional solidarity.[5] Namely, they demonstrate a critical self-awareness with an eye towards positional knowing, power asymmetries, and disparities in resources and representation. And they raise questions and concerns about the consequences of engagement in terms of outcome, and longevity.

Nurturing Practical Wisdom

Phronesis is a form of insight that enables right action. It requires more than the application of universals to particulars. It also requires the ability to understand, discern, appraise, and manage the complexities of specific situations all the while remaining critically aware of one's own positionality. Below I will break down the phronetic process into three modes of inquiry—contemplation, interpretation, and imagination—for you to use as touchstones on your path to practical wisdom. May they guide you well.

A mode of inquiry is the process by which a person acquires information, knowledge, understanding or, in this case, practical wisdom. The drawing below illustrates how the three modes of inquiry overlap, intersect, complement, and build on one another. While each constitutes a distinct modality, they are not hierarchical steps, or linear stages. You can move through them incrementally, simultaneously, recursively, slowly, or quickly. A person might be in one mode for a long time and another mode just briefly. Or they could repeat modes individually, sequentially, or in tandem. The idea is to use these modes of inquiry to cultivate insight and sharpen discernment. At the center, where the three circles intersect, is action. It represents the seedbed of practical wisdom. Together, these modes synthesize what I learned about the process of bringing peace through practical wisdom while writing this book.[6] I offer them as a set of lenses, not as a

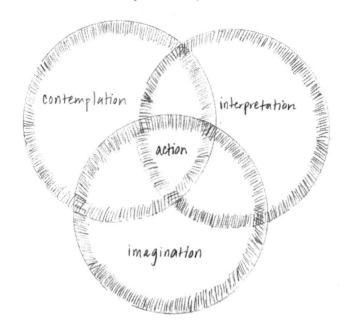

A Sketch of Practical Wisdom. Drawing from the author's notebook.

tried-and-true formula or method. A systematic procedure wouldn't make sense because phronesis is more art than science. Moving through these modes does not guarantee practical wisdom, but together they can help you stay awake, open-minded, and creatively maladjusted.[7]

Contemplation

If akrasia is deliberate avoidance, then contemplation is its opposite—acceptance and interest. Contemplation is fertile awareness, an openness to critical interruption and the call of consciousness. To contemplate is to open your aperture of attention to something real outside of the self. As a mode of inquiry contemplation is about observation and attunement. Contemplation asks, "What's going on?" and then listens without expectation. According to early twentieth century poet and novelist D. H. Lawrence: "an act of pure attention, if you are capable of it, will bring its own answer. And you choose that object to concentrate upon, which will best focus your consciousness."[8] When contemplation reaches the point of choice, that is, when the feelings that arise in you indicate that you need to decide where to focus your attention, then you are beginning to transition into interpretation. For now, let's continue to explore contemplation as its own mode inquiry.

Contemplation, mindfulness, and meditation have become increasingly popular buzzwords. During the global pandemic media outlets touted a mindfulness movement centered on practices associated with self-care that seek to improve a person's mental, physical, and emotional health.[9] Although I think these are good ideas, they are not what I mean by contemplation.

The type of contemplation I am referring to is a form of paying attention that has less to do with looking inward (self-consciousness) and more to do with looking outward (total consciousness). It works from the assumption that we are inextricably linked to everyone and everything in the world. Observing the self in this way, as part-to-whole, requires concentration and effort—like walking along a deep crevice carefully self-regulating while also acknowledging your (and by extension, others') inherent vulnerability. It is a perspective that can be developed through habituation.

Although contemplation requires concentration and effort, it does not rely on cognition or thought. Rather, it is a mode of inquiry that suspends thinking so we can pay attention to the world as it is, without concepts or stories.[10] At its best, contemplation is broad sustained vigilance but more realistically, it is an inquisitive disposition that fluctuates day to day and moment to moment in terms of its quality of attention. The point is to tune in and keep tuning in to what's going on around you. Before you can make sense of anything or imagine alternatives, you must first become aware.

Awareness draws from lived experience and the accumulation of knowledge. For example, you have to have a basic understanding of seasonality before you can meaningfully notice strawberries at the supermarket in February. This is, in part, why Aristotle considers practical wisdom to be a virtue of old age. In his words, "phronesis is concerned with particulars as well as universals, and particulars become known from experience, but a young person lacks experience, since some length of time is needed to produce it."[11] I understand his logic, but I disagree with his conclusion. What Aristotle ascribes to age I credit to exposure. Think of Keith Alaniz who went to war four times before he turned thirty (chapter 8). Attaching age to wisdom is a common stereotype and from the perspective of my interests in cultivating practical wisdom, it's limiting. In fact, I could argue the opposite—young people are more curious about the world and more open to taking risks and exposing themselves to new ideas and experiences.

A fundamental curiosity about the world is a prerequisite for contemplation. Curtis Romjue's story emphasized curiosity as a moral virtue associated with its Latin root, *cura* "care" (chapter 2) To be curious is to care. And to care means to pay attention, to notice, to be concerned or bothered.

Sometimes I prod my college students to write about what bothers them. I have found this to be a much more useful prompt than asking them to write about what interests them. Interests are fickle. The things that bother us, however, tend to share a common theme usually relating to universal values associated with justice, tolerance, dignity, equality, fairness, honesty, and respect. As a mode of inquiry, contemplation attunes us to what Romjue calls our heart's "resonant frequencies." In college, Romjue attended lectures and events, exposing himself to new information and ideas. That's how he learned about modern slavery. Then, he deepened his engagement with that subject through interpretation, imagination, and eventual action.

For Shannon Keith there's no alternative to tuning in; if you're not tuning in then you're tuning out (chapter 6). To tune out is to be like one of Plato's akrastic philosophers, giving up on justice and withdrawing from public life to avoid the friction of engagement. Contemplation, by contrast, is about accepting and paying attention to the friction, extending your antenna, not retracting it. Keith is an example of contemplation as broad sustained vigilance, always open to the call of conscience.

Interpretation

Interpretation involves making choices about where to focus your attention and becoming critical about your own positionality relative to the context of concern. If contemplation is general attunement, then interpretation is specific focus. "Focalization," writes nineteenth century philosopher William James, "implies withdrawal from some things in order to deal effectively with others."[12] Similarly Michael Hyde—the communication scholar I referred to in the last chapter in describing "the call of conscience"—argues that it is impossible for a finite being to respond to "all the others whose calls beg for acknowledgement" so, with every choice we make, we necessarily sacrifice obligations to respond "in the same way and in the same instance" to myriad others. Yet, respond we must because, as Hyde evocatively points out, "Imagine what life would be like if nobody acknowledged your existence."[13] Thus, as a mode of inquiry, interpretation relies on choice and judgment. It moves from "What is going on?" to "What do I make of it?"

Interpretation takes into account as much of the totality of a given situation as possible, including our own position in terms of power and agency. It means taking stock of "what we know, who we know, how we know it, and what works."[14] Interpretation draws from tacit knowledge, the knowledge you have gained from living your life. It is not a birds-eye-view, it is your view, which means your ability to understand (and misunderstand) shapes how you interpret what's going on.

To interpret, after all, is to translate. For example, about a decade ago I was a speech tutor for students who spoke English as a second (or third or fourth) language. One day, a student asked me what the word "trauma" meant. I remember giving a clumsy, rambling answer about painful experiences and memories. After a pause, the student said, "Oh, you mean like a shadow on the heart?" Not only did he catch my meaning, but his translation opened a whole new way of knowing for me. The cultural repertoire we have access to shapes our ability to make meaning, understand, and interpret. As a process, interpretation is beautifully imperfect because it embraces polysemy, the multiplicity of meaning, and accepts fundamental unknowability.[15] As a mode of inquiry, interpretation contextualizes what we do not know, and prompts us to ask more fertile and precise questions.

Interpretation differs from other ways of knowing due to its reliance on human judgment and context-based decision making. Other ways of knowing, especially in the technosciences, tend to circumscribe one problem and offer solutions without taking into account broader contexts. By contrast, interpretation tacks back and forth between broad and narrow perspectives, to accommodate new information and the indeterminacy of meaning. Compared to clinical, technoscientific approaches, interpretation seems messy and exhausting. What's more, as society becomes more complex, specialized, and bureaucratic, our akrastic tendencies flare and we find ourselves lured by what the technocrats call frictionless living.[16]

With so many demands on our attention, it is tempting to rely on algorithms, policies, rules and regulations to do the interpretive work for us. We hear the call of akrasia. "There are so many tragedies that need our involvement. Where do you begin?" asks Holocaust survivor Elie Wiesel. "A century ago, by the time the news of a war reached another place, the war was over," he writes, "Now people die, and the pictures of their dying are offered to you and to me while we are having dinner."[17] Wiesel goes on to ask how we might transform that knowledge into responsibility. I argue that it begins by moving from contemplation (awareness) to interpretation (making sense of).

It is not always a matter of rational, individual choice about where our obligations lie. Sometimes our obligations become apparent to us from seemingly out of nowhere. Shawn Lent noticed a lack of social infrastructure for refugees in her neighborhood (chapter 1). Estelle Brown noticed a lack of bugs on her windshield after an evening drive (chapter 4). Both did the work of interpreting what that meant and where they fit in.

Lent and Brown illustrate two different qualities of interpretation. Lent highlights interpretation as an iterative and recursive process. She observes, listens, and learns, then modifies her conceptual framework, and starts all over again. At every pass, she refines her understanding of the context and her responses to given situations become more tailored and specific. In contemplation she is receptive, in interpretation she is flexible. Brown's story foregrounds the role of emotions in drawing our attention to some things over others. Contemplation opens us up to being affected and our emotions direct us where to go. Even negative emotions are useful because they focus our attention, help us make choices, and motivate us to act. Brown's maladjusted feelings toward environmental issues and food insecurity prompted her to learn more about them as they pertain to her town. As a mode of inquiry in service to phronesis, interpretation functions to steady our gaze and locate the self within the context of concern.

Imagination

Imagination is about summoning possibility. If interpretation helps us grasp that which has already been done, the cut and dried paradigms at play, then imagination considers what it would mean to do something different, to act out, or mis-perform.[18] Imagination is future oriented, embracing the new and unrealized. But imagination is not dreaming, it is not a pie-in-the-sky, all-things-being-equal outlook. Rather, imagination is anchored to the sticky particulars of the present with all its hang-ups and constraints. In his writing on the moral imagination, John Paul Lederach describes it as the "capacity to imagine something rooted in the challenges of the real world yet capable of giving birth to that which does not yet exist."[19] As a mode of inquiry, imagination asks "What's possible?"

Imagination is crucial to future life. Without imagination, observes cultural critic Lewis Hyde, we would "never be led into new life" because we could only "spin the future out of the logic of the present."[20] Imagination helps us break free of normative thought patterns and habitual behavior.

Children have incredible imaginations. That is because their minds are unmuddied by convention. Children are new here; they're beginners, strangers. They don't yet have that voice in their heads telling them, "this is the right way" to use a spoon or get into a car seat. Instead, they experiment; doing what researchers call divergent thinking first and convergent thinking second. Put simply, divergent thinking is about imagination, drumming up all the possibilities and considering alternatives. "What happens if I scoop my yogurt with the handle?" "How does it feel to sit in my car seat backwards?" Then, they engage convergent thinking by making choices about which possibility works best. "I get more yogurt into my mouth if I use my spoon this way." "My arms are freer if I sit facing forward." As we grow up, divergent and convergent thinking (which happens in two different parts of the brain) compete with one another. When the divergent part kicks in and says, "hey, what if . . ." the convergent part responds almost immediately, "don't be silly." It's not that we lack the capacity to imagine, it's just that we don't often give ourselves permission to do it.[21]

Gidon Bromberg illustrates the value of taking a stranger's perspective (chapter 3). Having grown up outside of the Israeli-Palestinian conflict, he approached the environmental crisis with an almost childlike mind. "We share the same piece of Earth," he said. Zen Buddhists refer to this perspective as shoshin, a beginner's mind. A person with this mindset experiences the here and now without preconceived notions. Zen monk Shunryu Suzuki describes it as a "smooth, free-thinking way of observation—without stagnation."[22] When a person experiences something for the first time, they are more likely to test things out, make mistakes, and playfully explore possibilities. By contrast, when a mind is full of preconceived ideas, subjective intentions, or calcified habits, it is not as open to experimentation.[23] Think of Bromberg driving to meet his eventual collaborators for the first time. He said: "I certainly remember the butterflies in my stomach . . . I'm there, you know, 'is this dangerous what I'm doing?'" By applying his expertise as an environmental lawyer to a new situation in a novel way, Bromberg showcases the value of approaching a problem with divergent thinking first.

Outsiders, or people on the periphery of society are freer to imagine, innovate, and change because they are less concerned with being accepted.[24] Psychological research finds that minorities and misfits have an enhanced element of creativity called integrative complexity, meaning that they can reconcile conflicting information and feel less bothered by uncertainty.[25] Unusual experiences boost creativity because once you've experienced a violation of norms and see that the sky doesn't fall, you are more open to trying new things.[26]

All the people featured in this book share an element of weirdness. Not only are they all outsiders to the contexts in which they work, but their biographical experiences also contributed to their outsider-ness. At some point, each of them experienced themselves as Other in a way that allowed them to see social norms for what they are—constructions. This is a liberating revelation because it implies the possibility of change. If inhospitable aspects of society are mere constructions, then they can be deconstructed and replaced with more hospitable ones.

Toward that end, Nawal Rajeh and Ralph Moore made a series of unconventional choices in their own lives that led them to meeting each other and collaborating on Peace Camp (chapter 5). Collaboration is highly valuable to imagination and divergent thinking. Gaining access to the ideas and experiences of others expands creative potential. Moore had never heard of a peace camp before Rajeh came along. And without vocalizing her idea to Moore, Rajeh would never have received the permission and structural support she needed to do it. In Rajeh's words, "Don't be afraid to just say what your idea is and you'll find each other . . . when you speak that vision aloud or that idea or that deep hope to change the world aloud, you'll call people to you or you'll be called to them." Sometimes our capacity to imagine benefits from an audience more supportive than the critic inside our head.

Action

The three modes of inquiry—contemplation, interpretation, imagination—coalesce to form practical wisdom or right action. By moving recursively through the three modes of inquiry, a person may eventually arrive at a critical juncture where they find themselves in a position to be of benefit. It takes courage to act. It would be easier and safer not to do anything at all.

Let small action be an antidote to akrasia. Political theorist Hannah Arendt wrote, "the smallest act in the most limited circumstances bears the seed of . . . boundlessness, because one deed, and sometimes one word, suffices to change every constellation."[27] Think of Drew Matott's first small action—giving a book made from his deceased father's old blue jeans to his paternal uncle (chapter 7). "That experience right there with my uncle," said Matott, "really made me realize that papermaking and these processes that I was experiencing could have . . . a profound impact." From that experience, that small action, Matott built a career out of responding to the needs of others; first, combat veterans and, eventually, anyone who experienced pain or suffering.

With each small action, Matott moved recursively through the modes of inquiry. After he gave his uncle the book, he contemplated that experience. Then, he interpreted his positionality as someone who could facilitate a similar profound impact with others. Next, he imagined possibilities for what that could look like and acted on his vision by opening Green Door Studio. There, he met a combat veteran whose obvious pain prompted

Matott to contemplate, interpret, imagine, and act all over again and so on and so forth until all those right actions stack up into a life well-lived or what the ancient Greeks called eudaemonia, the good life and the telos of phronesis.

Feeling a responsibility to others moves us to action. According to philosopher Emmanuel Levinas, it is our ethical responsibility to show up for one another. Levinas, a Lithuanian Jew and the only one in his family to survive the Holocaust, developed a theory of intersubjective ethics grounded in our mutual obligations to each other. "I am he who finds the resources to respond to the call," writes Levinas.[28] Responses will vary, of course, and that's the point. Finding resources requires creativity, effort, and invention. Responding to the call is an opportunity to exercise practical wisdom. Each of us can contribute within the limits of our tether. This is how it's done—bit by bit, piece by piece.

The three modes of inquiry—contemplation (what's going on?), interpretation (what do I make of it?), and imagination (what's possible?)—help you recognize your ability to respond, your response-ability. Transforming that insight into action requires faith, courage, and commitment. Keith Alaniz knew very little about the spice trade in Afghanistan, yet he responded to the call nevertheless (chapter 8). "Start doing something, and it starts materializing before your eyes," he said. In other words, don't get hung up on an outcome. Don't worry about how you're going to get it done, just start.

Go in Peace

Now it's up to you, reader—Just start. The people in this book demonstrate—whether you find it profound, frustrating, or thrilling—it really is that simple. You can't know everything before you act. But you can move consciously through the world contemplating, interpreting, imagining, and offering your imperfect effort. To do that is to do peace through practical wisdom. I'll be over here doing my bit while you do yours. Here we go!

QUESTIONS FOR REFLECTION AND DISCUSSION

Which of the stories resonated with you? Why?

What is your definition of peace?

Where does wisdom come from?

When you give yourself solitude, or when your mind is idle, which ideas, issues, hopes, or topics draw your genuine attention?

To paraphrase a sentiment attributed to Audre Lorde, we tend to move where the chains chafe us the most. What does that mean for you? Where are you chafed? What bothers you?

Which life experiences have uniquely positioned you to recognize, know, or understand certain aspects of the world?

If you knew you couldn't fail, what would you most want to do for the world's benefit?

What is your definition of community? What kind of community nurtures and sustains you? What role do you play in creating and fostering community?

The author writes, "Sometimes our capacity to imagine benefits from an audience more supportive than the critic inside our head." Who is a safe and supportive audience for your ideas?

How would you answer peacebuilding scholar John Paul Lederach's "critical yeast" question? Who, if brought together in a given situation, would have the capacity to make things grow in a positive direction? What resources or support do you have?

Many of the stories reference the importance of a broader vision rather than specific action steps. Why do you think this vision is important?

The author writes, "The most practical thing to do is not always the most rational." What does she mean by this?

What keeps you from engaging? Describe the obstacles you face. Consider the three modes of inquiry—contemplation, interpretation, imagination—are you stuck in any one of them?

What does it mean to get results? To what extent is that a useful mindset? In what ways is it inhibiting?

NOTES

PREFACE

1. The word troubadour derives from modern French word trouver, which means to find, invent, or compose. I call upon the term here for its obvious relevance to folk music, but also for its emphasis on wayfinding and invention. Although we may never experience a folk music renaissance, we cannot afford to lose the troubadour spirit. It represents the human capacity for creativity and imagination.
2. Thomas Merton, *The Nonviolent Alternative* (New York: Farrar, Straus, and Giroux, 2010), 52.

INTRODUCTION

1. Chad Sokal and Rachel Sun. "Air quality 'unhealthy' in Spokane, North Idaho, Northeastern Washington" *The Spokesman-Review*, August 13, 2018. https://www.spokesman.com/stories/2018/aug/13/air-quality-unhealthy-in-spokane-north-idaho-north/.
2. Aaron Hegarty, "Timeline: Immigrant Children Separated from Families at the Border," *USA Today*, July 27, 2018, https://www.usatoday.com/story/news/2018/06/27/immigrant-children-family-separation-border-timeline/734014002/.
3. Carly Vandergreindt, "How Superhuman Strength Happens," *Healthline*, July 23, 2020, https://www.healthline.com/health/hysterical-strength#how-it-happens.
4. Jessica Gall Myrick, "Emotion Regulation, Procrastination, and Watching Cat Videos Online: Who Watches Internet Cats, Why, and to What Effect?" *Computers in Human Behavior* 52 (November 2015): 168–76.
5. Andrew Bacevich, "The Never-Ending War in Afghanistan," *New York Times*, March 13, 2017, https://www.nytimes.com/2017/03/13/opinion/.
6. Lisa Silvestri, "The Telling War Project," Gonzaga University College of Liberal Arts & Sciences, https://www.gonzaga.edu/college-of-arts-sciences/centers-initiatives/center-for-public-humanities/telling-war; National Endowment for the Humanities, "Telling War: Exploring Veteran Voices in Eastern Washington," NEH For All, https://nehforall.org/projects/; Shawn Vestal, "Veteran Turns a Page," *The Spokesman Review,* (May 27, 2019), https://www.spokesman.com/stories/2019/may/27/.
7. I am invoking Sly and the Family Stone's 1968 song, "Everyday People."
8. Cornel West, *The Radical King* (Boston, MA: Beacon Press, 2015).
9. Adrienne Rich, "Split at the Root: An Essay on Jewish Identity," in *Blood, Bread, and Poetry: Selected Prose 1979–1985* (New York: Norton, 1987), 123.
10. For an overview of the changing methodological landscape see Helene Snee, Christine Hine, Yvette Morey, Steven Roberts, and Hayley Watson, eds., *Digital Methods for Social Science: An Interdisciplinary Guide to Research Innovation* (New York: Palgrave Macmillan, 2016); Michael Keating, Bryan Rhodes, and Ashley

Richards, "Crowdsourcing: A Flexible Method for Innovation, Data Collection, and Analysis in Social Science Research," in *Social Media, Sociality, and Survey Research* (Hoboken, NJ: Wiley, 2013), 179–201; For epistemological implications see Alvin Tarrell, Nargess Tahmasbi, David Kocsis, Abhishek Tripathi, Jay Pedersen, Jie Xiong, Onook Oh, and Gert-Jan de Vreede, "Crowdsourcing: A Snapshot of Published Research" (presentation, Proceedings of the Nineteenth Americas Conference on Information Systems, August 15–17, 2013), https://aisel.aisnet.org/amcis2013/EndUserIS/GeneralPresentations/2.

11. A fuller version of his remark was "Remember outsourcing? Sending jobs to India and China is so 2003. The new pool of cheap labor: everyday people using their social circles to create content, solve problems, even do corporate R & D." Jeff Howe, "The Rise of Crowdsourcing," *Wired,* 14, no. 6 (2006), http://www.wired.com/wired/archive/14.06/crowds.html.

12. Lina Eklund, Isabell Stamm, and Wanda Katja Liebermann, "The Crowd in Crowdsourcing: Crowdsourcing as a Pragmatic Research Method," *First Monday* 24, no. 10 (2019), https://firstmonday.org/ojs/index.php/fm/article/view/9206/8124; See also Mark Hedges and Stuart Dunn, *Academic Crowdsourcing in the Humanities: Crowds, Communities and Co-production* (Cambridge, UK: Chandos Publishing, 2017); Enrique Estellés-Arolas, Fernando González-Ladrón-de-Guevara, "Towards an Integrated Crowdsourcing Definition," *Journal of Information Science* 38, no. 2 (2012): 189–200; Hana Shepherd, "Crowdsourcing," *Contexts* 11, no. 2 (2012): 10–11.

13. Daren C. Brabham, "The Myth of Amateur Crowds: A Critical Discourse Analysis of Crowdsourcing Coverage," *Information, Communication & Society* 15, no. 3 (2012): 394–410.

14. James Surowiecki, *The Wisdom of Crowds* (New York, NY: Anchor Books, 2005); Mark Wexler, "Reconfiguring the Sociology of the Crowd: Exploring Crowdsourcing," *International Journal of Sociology and Social Policy* 31, no. 1/2 (2011): 6–20.

15. For Gidon Bromburg and Shannon Keith, I used real-time video conferencing software.

16. Barney Glaser and Anselm Strauss, *Discovery of Grounded Theory: Strategies for Qualitative Research* (Chicago, IL: Aldine, 1967); Barney Glaser, *Theoretical Sensitivity: Advances in Methodology of Grounded Theory* (Mill Valley, CA: Sociological Press, 1978).

17. Lisa Ellen Silvestri, "Precarity, Nihilism, and Grace," *International Journal of Cultural Studies* 24, no. 2 (2021): 360–77.

18. Lisa Ellen Silvestri, "Standing Down, Standing Together: Coalition-Building at Standing Rock," *Rhetoric and Public Affairs* 26, no. 1 (2023): 73–100.

19. Walter Lippmann, *Drift and Mastery* (Madison: University of Wisconsin Press, 2015).

20. I am borrowing the word "drift" from Richard Sennet, *The Corrosion of Character* (New York: Norton, 1998).

21. There is more to postmodernity than markets and spheres, of course. Postmodernism is also the very feeling of drift itself; the melancholia and indifference that stem from what French Philosopher Jean Baudriallard calls the "disappearance of meaning." See Jean Baudrillard, *Simulacra and Simulation,* trans. Sheila Faria Glaser (Ann Arbor: University of Michigan Press, 1994), 163.

22. Adrian Franklin, "The Tourist Syndrome: An Interview with Zygmunt Bauman," *Tourist Studies* 3, no. 2 (2003): 208.

23. Whitney Phillips and Ryan Milner, *The Ambivalent Internet: Mischief, Oddity, and Antagonism Online* (Hoboken, NJ: Wiley, 2018), 53.

24. For articles on the internet-enabled public sphere see James Bohman, "Expanding Dialogue: The Internet, the Public Sphere and Prospects for Transnational Democracy," Sociological Review 52, no. 1 (2004): 131–55; Lincoln Dahlberg, "The Internet, Deliberative Democracy, and Power: Radicalizing the Public Sphere," International Journal of Media & Cultural Politics 3, no. 1 (2007): 47–64; Zizi Papacharissi, "The Virtual Sphere: The Internet as a Public Sphere," New Media & Society 4, no. 1 (2002): 9–27. For articles on political discourse online see Anthony Fung and Kent D. Kedl, "Representative Publics, Political Discourses and the Internet: A Case Study of a Degenerated Public Sphere in a Chinese Online Community," World Communication 29, no. 4 (2000): 69–84; Antje Gimmler, "Deliberative Democracy, the Public Sphere and the Internet," Philosophy & Social Criticism 27, no. 4 (2001): 21–39. For readings on organizing and activism see Clay Shirky, Here Comes Everybody: The Power of Organizing Without Organizations (New York: Penguin, 2008); Clay Shirky, "The Political Power of Social Media: Technology, the Public Sphere, and Political Change," Foreign Affairs 90, no. 1 (2011): 28–41. For the rise of polarization and hate speech see Jessie Daniels, "The Algorithmic Rise of the 'Alt-Right,'" Contexts 17, no. 1 (2018): 60–65; Merlyna Lim, "Freedom to Hate: Social Media, Algorithmic Enclaves, and the Rise of Tribal Nationalism in Indonesia," Critical Asian Studies 49, no. 3 (2017): 411–27; Whitney Phillips and Ryan M. Milner, You Are Here: A Field Guide for Navigating Polarized Speech, Conspiracy Theories, and Our Polluted Media Landscape (Cambridge, MA: MIT Press, 2021); Sara Polak and Daniel Trottier, "Introducing Online Vitriol," Violence and Trolling on Social Media: History, Affect, and Effects on Online Vitriol (Amsterdam, The Netherlands: Amsterdam University Press, 2020), 9; Heather Suzanne Woods, "Anonymous, Steubenville, and the Politics of Visibility: Questions of Virality and Exposure in the Case of #OPRollRedRoll and #OccupySteubenville," Feminist Media Studies 14, no. 6 (2014): 1096–98.

25. Zygmunt Bauman, *Liquid Modernity* (Cambridge, UK: Polity Press, 2000), 38.

26. Papacharissi described "privately public conversations" and "affective publics" as attributes of the new public spheres in Zizi A. Papacharissi, *A Private Sphere: Democracy in a Digital Age* (Cambridge, UK: Polity, 2010) and in *Affective Publics: Sentiment, Technology, and Politics* (London: Oxford University Press, 2015).

27. Book VII of Aristotle, *Aristotle: Nicomachean Ethics*, 2nd ed. trans. Terence Irwin (Indianapolis, IN: Hackett, 1999).

28. The idea that someone would knowingly do something bad is considered the Socratic paradox. For thorough treatments on the concept of akrasia, especially Socrates's denial of it, read John Mouracade, "Pleasure, Desire, and *Akrasia* in Plato's *Republic*," *Méthexis* 28, no. 1 (2016): 33–46; Christopher Bobonich and Pierre Destree, eds. *Akrasia in Greek Philosophy: From Socrates to Plotinus* (Leiden, The Netherlands: Koninklijke Brill NV, 2007).

29. Plato, *The Republic*, ed. G. R. F. Ferrari, trans. Tom Griffith (New York: Cambridge University Press, 2007), 195.

30. There is a famous Italian Renaissance painting (a fresco) depicting "The School of Athens" where Plato and Aristotle appear in the center walking toward us, engaged in a dialogue we cannot hear. The older of the two, Plato, with a white beard, points an index finger skyward while his student Aristotle gestures with an

open palm pressing down to the earth. I always liked this image, believing that they were discussing the tenets of practical wisdom and the dance between the real and the ideal, the timeless, and the timely.

31. Dewey's critique of Aristotle mirrors my own of Bauman. Both thinkers exhibit a preference for fixity. In Bauman, it expresses itself as nostalgia for the good old "solid" days. See John Dewey, *Experience and Nature* (Chicago, IL: Open Court, 1925), 48.

32. The notion of moral jazz highlights a person's relationship to convention, rules, and procedure by insisting on agency because what makes jazz music is not just the notes on the page, but how a musician deviates from the notes on the page. See Barry Schwartz, "Practical Wisdom and Organizations," *Research in Organizational Behavior* 31 (2011): 3–23; Barry Schwartz and Kenneth Sharpe. *Practical Wisdom: The Right Way to Do the Right Thing* (New York: Penguin, 2011), 42–43.

33. Robert Hariman, "Prudence/Performance," *Rhetoric Society Quarterly* 21, no. 2 (1991): 26.

34. Aristotle, *Aristotle: Nicomachean Ethics*, 2nd ed. trans. Terence Irwin (Indianapolis, IN: Hackett, 1999).

35. Thomas Farrell, *Norms of Rhetorical Culture* (New Haven, CT: Yale University Press, 1995), 97.

36. Maxine Greene, "Teaching in a Moment of Crisis: The Spaces of Imagination," *New Educator* 1, no. 2 (2005): 79.

37. Václav Havel, *Disturbing the Peace: A Conversation with Karel Hvizdala*, trans. Paul Wilson (New York: Vintage Books, 1990), 181–82.

38. As referenced by Keith Holyoak, *The Spider's Thread: Metaphor in Mind, Brain, and Poetry* (Cambridge, MA: The MIT Press, 2019): 29.

39. Gayatri Spivak, "Can the Subaltern Speak?" in *Marxism and the Interpretation of Culture,* ed. Larry Grossberg and Cary Nelson (Houndmills, UK: Macmillan, 1998), 66–111.

40. Simone Weil, *Gravity and Grace,* trans. A. Wills (Lincoln: University of Nebraska Press, 1997): 333.

41. Martin Luther King Jr. "Letter from The Birmingham City Jail," Public Domain, April 16, 1963, https://www.africa.upenn.edu/Articles_Gen/Letter_Birmingham.html.

42. Kimberlé Crenshaw, "Mapping the Margins: Intersectionality, Identity Politics, and Violence against Women of Color," *Stanford Law Review* 43, no. 6 (1991): 1241–99.

43. Patricia Hill Collins, and Sirma Bilge, *Intersectionality* (Hoboken, NJ: Wiley, 2020); Jennifer C. Nash, "Re-thinking Intersectionality," *Feminist Review* 89, no. 1 (2008): 1–15.

44. Adrienne Rich, *Blood, Bread, and Poetry: Selected Prose 1979–1985* (New York: Norton, 1986), 219; Aimee Carrillo Rowe, "Be Longing: Toward a Feminist Politics of Relation," *NWSA Journal,* 17, no. 2 (2005): 15–46.

45. Zygmunt Bauman, *Intimations of Postmodernity* (New York: Routledge, 2003); Anthony Giddens, *Modernity and Self Identity* (Cambridge, UK: Polity Press, 1991).

46. Martha Nussbaum, "Education for Citizenship in an Era of Global Connection," *Studies in Philosophy and Education* 21, no. 4 (2002): 289–303; Marinus Ossewaarde, "Cosmopolitanism and the Society of Strangers," *Current Sociology* 55, no. 3 (2007): 367–88.

47. Stuart Hall, "New Ethnicities" in *Stuart Hall: Critical Dialogue in Cultural Studies,* ed. David Morley and Kuan-Hsing Chen (London and New York: Routledge, 1996), 442–51.
48. Elaine Almeida and Lisa Silvestri, "Feeding the Civic Imagination (Part One): Intercultural Food," *Henry Jenkins* (blog), May 18, 2022, http://henryjenkins.org/blog/2022/5/8/.
49. Georg Simmel, *The Sociology of Georg Simmel* trans. and ed., with introduction, Kurt H. Wolff (New York: Free Press, 1950).
50. Alfred Schütz, "The Stranger: An Essay in Social Psychology," *American Journal of Sociology* 49, no. 6 (1944): 499–507.
51. Julia Kristeva, *Strangers to Ourselves* (New York: Columbia University Press, 1991).
52. À la Simone Weil and Michel Foucault, self-critique involves interrogating how one's own subjectivity relates to others, and how normative systems of power enable and constrain the self. See: Simone Weil, *First and Last Notebooks* (Oxford: Oxford University Press, 1970) and Michel Foucault, "What is Critique" pp. 41–81 in *The Politics of Truth*, eds. Sylvere Lotringer and Lysa Hochroth, (The MIT Press, 2007).
53. Iris Murdoch, *The Sovereignty of Good* (New York: Routledge, 2013), 5, 82.
54. Robin Wall Kimmerer, *Braiding Sweetgrass: Indigenous Wisdom, Scientific Knowledge and the Teachings of Plants* (Minneapolis, MN: Milkweed Editions, 2013), 6.
55. Kent Hoffman, Glen Cooper, Bert Powell, and Christine M. Benton *Raising a Secure Child* (New York: Guilford Press, 2017), 17.

CHAPTER 1: TRUST YOUR PARTNERS

1. Violence in Syria involves fighting among several different factions—the Syrian Armed Forces (and its domestic and international allies including Iran, Russia, and Hezbollah), Turkish-backed Sunni opposition rebel groups, Kurdish, Arab, and Assyrian/Syriac militias, Salafi jihadist groups, and the Islamic State of Iraq and the Levant (ISIL).
2. Iraq has become more stable in recent years, especially with the formation of a new government in 2020. For the context that produced refugees like Lent's dance student, see Kathryn Libel, and Scott Harding, "Humanitarian Alliances: Local and International NGO Partnerships and the Iraqi Refugee Crisis," *Journal of Immigrant & Refugee Studies* 9, no. 2 (2011): 162–78.
3. Syeda Naushin Parnini, Mohammad Redzuan Othman, and Amer Saifude Ghazali, "The Rohingya Refugee Crisis and Myanmar-Bangladesh Relations," *Asian and Pacific Migration Journal* 22, no. 1 (2013): 137, https://doi.org/10.1177/011719681302200107.
4. Burt Feintuch, "Longing for Community," *Western Folklore* 60, no. 2 (2001): 149. See also Dorothy Noyes, "Façade Performances: Public Face, Private Mask," *Southern Folklore* 52, no. 2 (1995): 91.
5. Richard Bauman, "Differential Identity and the Social Base of Folklore," *Journal of American Folklore* 84, no. 331 (1971): 31–41.
6. After Morsi's government announced a temporary constitutional declaration that, in effect, granted the president unlimited powers.
7. Rainer Maria Rilke, *Rilke's Book of Hours: Love Poems to God,* trans. Anita Barrows and Joanna Macy (New York: Riverhead Books, 2005), 45.

CHAPTER 2: KNOW YOUR LIMITS

1. Christine Gregoire was the 22nd governor of Washington from 2005 to 2013, the second female to serve in the role.
2. "Strange Fruit" was written during a decade when activist organizations such as the National Association for the Advancement of Colored People were pressing lawmakers to make lynching a federal crime. As of this writing, lynching is still not considered a federal crime. The most recent attempt to make it so occurred in 2020. See Jacey Fortin, "Congress Moves," *New York Times,* February 26, 2020, https://www.nytimes.com/2020/02/26/us/politics/anti-lynching-bill.html.
3. Nicole Crowder, "Child Victims of Sexual Abuse in Guatemala are Giving Birth at Alarming Rates," *Washington Post,* August 19, 2015, https://www.washingtonpost.com/news/in-sight/wp/2015/08/19/.
4. In 2015, an estimated 12 million adult coloring books were sold in the United States, according to Nielsen Bookscan.
5. Dick Startz, "Teacher Pay Around the World," *Brown Center Chalkboard,* June 20, 2018, https://www.brookings.edu/articles/teacher-pay-around-the-world/.
6. Ranier Maria Rilke, trans. Anita Barrows and Joanna Macy, *Rilke's Book of Hours: Love Poems to God* (New York: Riverhead Books, 1996), 45.
7. "What We Offer," *First Aid Arts,* accessed April 4, 2024, https://www.firstaidarts.org/trainings-and-workshops.
8. Theologian Frederick Buechner defines vocation as the place where "your deep gladness and the world's deep hunger meet" in Frederick Buechner, *Wishful Thinking: A Seeker's ABCs* (New York: HarperOne, 1993), 118.
9. Elias Baumgarten, "Curiosity as a Moral Virtue," *International Journal of Applied Philosophy* 15, no. 2 (2001): 173.
10. Martin Luther King Jr., "I Have a Dream," August 28, 1963, *A Testament of Hope: The Essential Writings and Speeches Martin Luther King Jr.* (New York: HarperOne, 1986), 218.
11. Martin Luther King Jr., "I See the Promised Land," April 3, 1968, *A Testament of Hope: The Essential Writings and Speeches Martin Luther King Jr.* (New York: HarperOne, 1986, 54.

CHAPTER 3: SEE FROM THE OUTSIDE

1. David M. Halbfinger and Iyad Abuheweila, "One Dead Amid Violence in 3rd Week of Protests at Gaza-Israel Fence" *New York Times,* April 13, 2018, https://www.nytimes.com/2018/04/13/world/middleeast/gaza-israel-protests.html; Khaled Abu Toameh, "Hamas Vows Gaza Protests Last until Palestinians Return to All of Palestine," *Times of Israel,* April 9, 2018, https://www.timesofisrael.com/.
2. Mark Landler, "Trump Recognizes Jerusalem as Israel's Capital and Orders U.S. Embassy to Move," *New York Times,* December 6, 2017, https://www.nytimes.com/2017/12/06/world/middleeast/.
3. Bromberg's accolades include the prestigious Skoll Award for Social Entrepreneurship, Stanford University's Bright Award for the Environment, the Mother Teresa Memorial Award for Social Justice, and in 2008, *Time* magazine named him an Environmental Hero.
4. The Nagorno-Karabakh conflict is an ethnic territorial battle between Armenia and Azerbaijan over the disputed region in Afghanistan ongoing since the late 1980s. See Ken Conca and Jennifer Wallace, "Environment and Peacebuilding in War-torn Societies: Lessons from the UN Environment Programme's Experience

with Postconflict Assessment," *Global Governance: A Review of Multilateralism and International Organizations* 15, no. 4 (2009): 485–504.

5. Intifada refers to a period of sustained protest and violent revolt among Palestinians against Israeli occupation of the West Bank and Gaza. The First Intifada in the late 1980s to the early 1990 lasted about six years. The Second, in the early 2000s, sustained itself for an estimated four years. President Donald Trump's 2017 decision to move the US embassy from Tel Aviv to Jerusalem inspired rumblings for a Third Intifada.

6. The Dead Sea is roughly 30 miles long and 9 miles wide. See Ittai Gayrieli, Amos Bien, and Aharon Oren, "The Expected Impact of the Peace Conduit Project (The Red Sea – Dead Sea Pipeline) on the Dead Sea," *Mitigation and Adaptation Strategies for Global Change.* 10 (2005): 3–22.

7. For Bromberg's earliest published research on peace, see Alon Tal, Shoshana Lopatin, and Gidon Bromberg, "Sustainability of Energy-Related Development Projects in the Middle East Peace Region." (1995), https://pdf.usaid.gov/pdf_docs/PNABY020.pdf.

8. The current EcoPeace leadership is Gidon Bromberg (Israel), Yana Abu Taleb (Jordan), and Nada Majdalani (Palestine).

9. Oliver Holmes, "Israel and Palestine: What Has Caused Violence to Flare Up Again," *The Guardian,* January 30, 2023, https://www.theguardian.com/world/2023/jan/30/.

10. "Civil Society Speakers Paint Grim Picture of Deepening Crisis in Occupied Palestinian Territory, as Security Council Takes Up Middle East Situation," *The United Nations.* April 19, 2019, https://press.un.org/en/2019/sc13794.doc.htm.

11. Victor W. Turner, "Betwixt and Between: The Liminal Period in Rites de Passage," in *The Forest of Symbols: Aspects of Ndembu Ritual,* ed. V. W. Turner (Ithaca, NY: Cornell University Press, 1967), 9.

12. Paul Radin, *The Trickster: A Study in American Indian Mythology* (New York: Philosophical Library, 1956).

13. Kamala Visweswaran, *Fictions of Feminist Ethnography* (Minneapolis, MN: University of Minnesota Press, 1994), 100.

14. Lewis Hyde, *Trickster Makes This World: Mischief, Myth, and Art* (New York: North Point. 1998).

CHAPTER 4: EMBRACE MALADJUSTMENT

1. John Paull, "'Please Pick Me'—How Incredible Edible Todmorden is Repurposing the Commons for Open Source Food and Agricultural Biodiversity," in *Diversifying Foods and Diets: Using Agricultural Biodiversity to Improve Nutrition and Health,* ed. J. Franzo, D. Hunter, T. Borelli, and F. Mattei (Oxford: Earthscan, New York: Routledge, 2013), 336–45.

2. Lindsay M. Chervinsky, "Vietnam War Protests at the White House," *The White House Historical Association,* https://www.whitehousehistory.org/.

3. Prior to the Industrial Revolution, Todmorden was a sleepy, wool-producing village surrounded by vast moorlands. "Welcome to Todmorden," *Todmorden Information Centre,* accessed April 4, 2024, https://www.visittodmorden.co.uk/

4. Serena Bartys, "Todmorden's Vital Signs," Calderdale's Vital Signs Report: A Guide to Local Charitable Giving, 2015, https://www.incredible-edible-todmorden.co.uk/blogs/.

5. Pants is British slang for bad and refers to underwear. A person might say "That's pants" or "a pile of pants" to communicate dislike.

6. Chris Osterndorf, "10 Reasons Wal-Mart is the Worst Company in America," *Salon,* May 25, 2015, https://www.salon.com/2015/05/25/.

7. A 2017 survey found that Incredible Edible Todmorden has had the largest impact on young children, but all age demographics have benefitted from its existence. For example, 80 percent of survey respondents had visited the Incredible Edible stand at a local food event, 27 percent had participated in planting activities, and 70 percent of respondents reported increases in food growing knowledge, understanding of community issues, understanding of environmental issues, understanding of local economic issues, activeness, and physical health. For the complete summary report, see Adrian Morley, Alan Farrier, and Mark Dooris, "Propogating Success: An Evaluation of the Social, Environment, and Economic Impacts of the Incredible Edible Todmorden Initiative," https://www.incredibleedible.org.uk/wp-content/uploads/2018/06/.

8. Audre Lorde, "The Uses of Anger." *Women's Studies Quarterly* 9, no. 3 (1981): 7–10.

9. Aristotle devoted a whole chapter to emotions in *Rhetoric.*

10. Karen Tracy, "Reasonable Hostility: Its Usefulness and Limitation as a Norm for Public Hearings," *Informal Logic* 31, no. 3(2011): 171–90.

11. "Transcript of Dr. Martin Luther King's speech at SMU on March 17, 1966," SMU Archives, January 10, 2014, https://www.smu.edu/News/2014/; "King's Challenge to the Nation's Social Scientists," *American Psychological Association,* September 1967, https://www.apa.org/monitor/features/.

12. Simone Weil makes a similar distinction between pity and compassion in Simone Weil, *On Science, Necessity and the Love of God,* trans. Richard Rees (London: Oxford University Press, 1968). She says pity consists of helping someone in misfortune so you are not obliged to think about them anymore and compassion means identifying with an other so fully that you feed them for the same reason you feed yourself: you are both hungry.

CHAPTER 5: SPEAK UP

1. The full quote by Sartre is "it's on the day that we can conceive of a different state of affairs that a new light falls on our troubles and our suffering and that we decide that these are unbearable," as cited in Maxine Greene, *Releasing the Imagination: Essays on Education, the Arts, and Social Change* (Hoboken, NJ: Wiley, 2000), 5.

2. At the time of this writing, Peace Camp's doors have been open for sixteen years, and has served almost a thousand Baltimore families.

3. Substance Abuse and Mental Health Services Administration, "Youth Violence: A Report of the Surgeon General," https://pubmed.ncbi.nlm.nih.gov/20669522/.

4. Freddie Gray is a 25-year-old man who died in 2015 from spinal cord injuries that he sustained while in police custody.

5. National Center for Education Statistics, "Undergraduate Degree Fields," Condition of Education 2022 Report, US Department of Education, Institute of Education Sciences, https://nces.ed.gov/programs/coe/indicator/cta.

6. Martin Luther King Jr., "I've Been to the Mountaintop," Mason Temple, April 3, 1968, Memphis Tennessee, transcript retrieved December 9, 2020, https://www.americanrhetoric.com/speeches/.

7. Julian Baggini, *Philosophy: Key Texts* (New York: Palgrave Macmillan, 2016), 14.

8. Aristotle, *Nicomachean Ethics.* 2nd ed. trans. Terence Irwin (Indianapolis, IN: Hackett, 1999).

CHAPTER 6: TAKE RISKS

1. Robert Gregg, "Unreal Cities: Bombay, London, New York," *Radical History Review* 70, no. 1 (1998): 131–48; Mona Rana, "Meeting Pakistani Prostitutes," *BBC News,* August 31, 2009, http://news.bbc.co.uk/2/hi/south_asia/8222222.stm.

2. US Department of State, "2018 Trafficking in Persons Report: India," https://www.state.gov/reports/.

3. As Shira Chess argues, even the most routine shopping activities are "significant, deep, creative, laden with responsibilities, and richly polysemic with diverse meanings." See Shira Chess, *The Motherhood Business: Consumption, Communication, and Privilege* (Tuscaloosa: University of Alabama Press, 2015), 9. For more critical consumer studies see Mary Douglas and Baron Isherwood, *The World of Goods* (New York: Basic Books, 1979); Daniel Miller, *Material Culture and Mass Consumption* (Oxford, UK: Basil Blackwell, 1987); John Sloop, "People Shopping," in *Rhetoric, Materiality, & Politics,* ed. Barbara A Biesecker and John Louis Lucaties (New York: Peter Lang, 2009), 67–98; Roopali Mukherjee and Sarah Banet-Weiser, *Commodity Activism: Cultural Resistance in Neoliberal Times* (New York: New York University Press, 2012).

4. Kenneth Burke, *Language as Symbolic Action* (Berkeley: University of California Press, 1966), 16.

5. Burke, *Language as Symbolic Action,* 60.

6. In his famous book, *The 7 Habits of Highly Effective People* (New York: Simon & Schuster, 1991), Stephen Covey explores three spheres—concern, influence, and control. The sphere of concern has to do with the wide range of worries we might have about a subject, the sphere of influence narrows the first by focusing on what we can do about our concerns, and the third is an even smaller sphere representing the things we can directly do something about.

7. I borrow the term "inner certainty" from Polish poet, Czeslaw Milosz. See his autobiographical essays: Czeslaw Milosz, *To Begin Where I Am: Selected Essays* (New York: Macmillan, 2002).

8. Lucille Clifton, "Conversations," *Rattle* (Winter 2002): 149.

CHAPTER 7: CREATE SPACE

1. The phrase "rags to riches" originated during the eighteenth century when the price of rags soared due to the invention of the printing press and subsequent increased demand for paper.

2. Rainer Maria Rilke, *Rilke's Book of Hours: Love Poems to God,* trans. Anita Barrows and Joanna Macy (New York: Riverhead Books, 2005), 119.

3. If you like some of these ideas, you might enjoy: Lewis Hyde, *The Gift: How the Creative Spirit Transforms the World* (New York: Vintage, 2019). Hyde describes a gift economy as a system of exchange that values relationships over commodities.

4. Ann Mongoven, *Just Love: Transforming Civic Virtue* (Bloomington: Indiana University Press, 2009), 16. For more on trust, vulnerability, and inherent interdependence, read one of my favorites Lauren Berlant, "A Properly Political Concept

of Love: Three Approaches in Ten Pages," *Cultural Anthropology* 26, no. 4 (2011): 683–91.

5. Ann Mongoven, "Integrity versus Impartiality: Healing a False Dichotomy," *Journal of the Society of Christian Ethics* 24, no. 2 (Fall/Winter 2004): 49. See also Diana Fritz Cates, *Choosing to Feel: Virtue, Friendship, and Compassion for Friends* (Notre Dame, IN: University of Notre Dame Press, 1997), especially chapter 6.

CHAPTER 8: THINK BIG, STEP SMALL

1. Associated Press, "U.S. Soldiers in Iraq Still Buying Their Own Body Armor," *Billings Gazette,* March 26, 2004, https://billingsgazette.com/; Michael Moss, "Many Missteps Tied to Delay of Armor to Protect Soldiers," *New York Times,* March 7, 2005, https://www.nytimes.com/2005/03/07/world/middleeast/.

2. Michael Moss, "Pentagon Study Links Fatalities to Body Armor," *New York Times,* January 7, 2006, https://www.nytimes.com/2006/01/07/politics/.

3. Jason Shell, "How the IED Won: Dispelling the Myth of Tactical Success and Innovation," *War on the Rocks,* May 1, 2017, https://warontherocks.com/2017/05/.

4. James Hosek and Paco Martorell, "How Have Deployments During the War on Terrorism Affected Reenlistment?" *RAND National Defense Research Institute,* 2009, https://www.rand.org/pubs/monographs/MG873.html.

5. According to the United States Embassy in Kabul, 80 percent of the Afghan population works in agriculture, https://af.usembassy.gov/.

6. Rhetorical scholar Thomas Farrell argues that critical interruptions promote rhetorical invention. See Thomas Farrell, *Norms of Rhetorical Culture* (New Haven, CT: Yale University Press, 1993), 258.

7. Hyde, Michael J. "The Call of Conscience: Heidegger and the Question of Rhetoric," *Philosophy & Rhetoric* 27, no.4 (1994): 379.

8. Phaedra Pezzullo argues that critical interruptions make an implicit call for a new ending. See Phaedra Pezzullo, "Performing Critical Interruptions: Stories, Rhetorical Invention, and the Environmental Justice Movement," *Western Journal of Communication* 65, no.1 (2001): 1–25.

9. Christopher Kolenda, *Zero-Sum Victory: What We're Getting Wrong About War* (Lexington: University Press of Kentucky, 2021).

10. Moral certitudes appear as "thou shalt nots" because it's easier to identify negative action than it is to imagine positive action.

11. John Paul Lederach, *The Moral Imagination: The Art and Soul of Building Peace,* (London: Oxford University Press, 2005).

CONCLUSION

1. John Steinbeck, *The Log from the Sea of Cortez* (New York: Penguin Books, 1951), 15.

2. Jesuit priest and scholar Michel de Certeau also uses this metaphor in Michel de Certeau, *The Practice of Everyday Life,* trans. S. Rendall (Berkeley: University of California Press, 1984). His work has greatly influenced my thoughts over the years.

3. I like feminist scholar Cheryl Glenn's definition of eudaemonia as "the well-being that comes from a lifetime of right habits and wise choices." See Cheryl Glenn, *Rhetorical Feminism and This Thing Called Hope* (Carbondale: Southern Illinois Press, 2018), 165.

4. Aristotle, *Nicomachean Ethics*, 2nd ed. book 5, chapter 1, trans. Terence Irwin (Indianapolis, IN: Hackett, 1999).
5. For scholarship on intersectional solidarity, see Rachel L. Einwohner, Kaitlin Kelly-Thompson, Valeria Sinclair-Chapman, Fernando Tormos-Aponte, S. Laurel Weldon, Jared M.Wright, and Charles Wu, "Active Solidarity: Intersectional Solidarity in Action," *Social Politics: International Studies in Gender, State, & Society* 28, no. 3 (2021): 704–29; Aimee Carrillo Rowe, *Power lines: On the Subject of Feminist Alliances* (Durham, NC: Duke University Press, 2008); Lisa Silvestri, "Standing Down, Standing Together: Coalition-Building at Standing Rock," *Rhetoric & Public Affairs* 23, no. 1 (2023): 73–100; Fernando Tormos, "Intersectional Solidarity," *Politics, Groups, and Identities* 5, no. 4 (2017): 707–20.
6. In some ways, the book you hold in your hands is an outcome of this triad. My early concept for the book came from asking myself, "What's possible?" (imagination), the interviews and the stories in each chapter are the results of mediated contemplation, the reflections after each chapter are my interpretations, and the preparation and publication of the book is my form of action.
7. I am invoking King's concept of creative maladjustment again here. I also love Maxine Greene's concept of wide-awakeness in Maxine Greene, "Wide-Awakeness and the Moral Life," in *Exploring Education,* (New York: Routledge, 2017), 219–24. See also Paulo Freire and Robert Barr, *Pedagogy of Hope: Reliving Pedagogy of the Oppressed* (London: Continuum International Publishing Group, 2004).
8. David Herbert Lawrence, *Sketches of Etruscan Places and Other Italian Essays* (New York: Cambridge University Press, 2002), 62.
9. Kira Cooper, "Practicing Mindfulness Can Help Us Through the Coronavirus Pandemic," *The Conversation,* July 5, 2020, https://theconversation.com/practising -mindfulness-can-help-us-through-the-coronavirus-pandemic-140617; Harvard Medical School, "Mindfulness Can Improve Mental Health During and After the COVID-19 Crisis," *Harvard Medical School Primary Care Review,* July 10, 2020, https://info.primarycare.hms.harvard.edu/review/mindfulness-during-after -covid; Shelly Tygielski, "Rethinking Our Self-Care During the Pandemic," *Mindful,* March 31, 2020, https://www.mindful.org/.
10. If you like these ideas, consider reading Robert Zeretsky, *The Subversive Simone Weil: A Life in Five Ideas* (Chicago, IL: University of Chicago Press, 2021).
11. Aristotle, *Nicomachean Ethics,* 2nd ed. book 6, chapter 9, trans. Terence Irwin (Indianapolis, IN: Hackett, 1999).
12. William James, *Principles of Psychology* (New York: Holt, 1890), 381–84.
13. Michael Hyde, "The Call of Conscience: Heidegger and the Question of Rhetoric," *Philosophy & Rhetoric* 27, no. 4 (1994): 379.
14. Cheryl Glenn calls a similar interpretive process, "strategic contemplation," in Cheryl Glenn, *Rhetorical Feminism and This Thing Called Hope* (Carbondale: Southern Illinois Press, 2018), 190.
15. As the mystic philosopher Simone Weil points out, "It does not even matter much whether we succeed in finding the solution or understanding the proof, although it is important to try really hard to do so. Never in any case whatever is a genuine effort of the attention wasted." Simone Weil, *Waiting for God* (New York: GP Putnam's Sons, 1951), 106.
16. Jakko Kemper, "The Environment and Frictionless Technology," *Media Theory* 6, no. 2 (2022): 55–76; Robert Payne, "Frictionless Sharing and Digital Promiscuity,"

Communication and Critical/Cultural Studies 11, no. 2 (2014): 85–102; Heather Suzanne Woods, "Asking More of Siri and Alexa: Feminine Persona in Service of Surveillance Capitalism," *Critical Studies in Media Communication* 35, no. 4 (2018): 334–49.

17. Elie Wiesel and Richard Heffner, *Conversations with Elie Wiesel* (New York: Knopf Doubleday Publishing Group, 2009), 4. Wiesel also gave a celebrated speech on the same theme called "The Perils of Indifference," *The History Place: Great Speeches Collection,* March 1, 2008, http://www.historyplace.com/speeches/wiesel .htm.

18. Although misperformance is a relatively widely used concept today, I want to cite my introduction to it Judith Butler, *Bodies That Matter: On the Discursive Limits of Sex* (New York: Routledge, 1993) and Judith Butler *Gender Trouble: Feminism and the Subversion of Identity,* 10th ed. (New York: Routledge, 1999).

19. John Paul Lederach, *The Moral Imagination: The Art and Soul of Building Peace* (London: Oxford University Press, 2005), ix.

20. Lewis Hyde, *The Gift: How the Creative Spirit Transforms the World* (New York: Vintage Books, 1983), 252.

21. This is in part a symptom of our education system's reliance on standardized testing, but I digress. For research on divergent and convergent thinking see Herie B. de Vries and Todd I. Lubart, "Scientific Creativity: Divergent and Convergent Thinking and the Impact of Culture," *Journal of Creative Behavior* 53, no. 2 (2019): 145–55; Weitao Zhang, Zsuzsika Sjoerds, and Bernhard Hommel, "Metacontrol of Human Creativity: The Neurocognitive Mechanisms of Convergent and Divergent Thinking," *NeuroImage* 210 (2020): 116572, https://www.sciencedirect.com/ science/article/pii/S1053811920300598.

22. Shunryu Suzuki, *Zen Mind, Beginner's Mind: Informal Talks on Zen Meditation and Practice* (Shambhala Publications, 2010), 105.

23. Suzuki, *Zen Mind,* 77; In the rhetorical tradition, Kenneth Burke describes a similar phenomenon as a trained incapacity, when "one's very abilities can function as blindnesses," in Kenneth Burke, *Permanence and Change: An Anatomy of Purpose* (Berkeley: University of California Press, 1984), 7

24. Patricia Hill Collins, "Learning from the Outsider Within: The Sociological Significance of Black Feminist Thought," *Social problems* 33, no. 6 (1986): s14–s32; Jonah Lehrer, *Imagine: How Creativity Works* (Boston, MA: Houghton Mifflin Harcourt, 2012); Susan Rubin Suleiman, ed., *Exile and Creativity: Signposts, Travelers, Outsiders, Backward Glances* (Durham, NC: Duke University Press, 1998).

25. Deborah H. Gruenfeld, Melissa C. Thomas-Hunt, and Peter H. Kim, "Cognitive Flexibility, Communication Strategy, and Integrative Complexity in Groups: Public versus Private Reactions to Majority and Minority Status," *Journal of Experimental Social Psychology* 34, no. 2 (1998): 202–26; Dacher Keltner, Deborah H. Gruenfeld, and Cameron Anderson, "Power, Approach, and Inhibition," *Psychological Review* 110, no. 2 (2003): 265l; Carsten K. W. De Dreu and Michael A. West, "Minority Dissent and Team Innovation: The Importance of Participation in Decision Making," *Journal of Applied Psychology* 86, no. 6 (2001): 1191.

26. Scott Barry Kaufman and Carolyn Gregoire, *Wired to Create: Unraveling the Mysteries of the Creative Mind* (New York: Penguin, 2016).

27. Hannah Arendt, *The Human Condition* (Chicago, IL: University of Chicago Press, 1998), 190.

28. Emmanuel Levinas, *Totality and Infinity, An Essay on Exteriority,* trans. Alphonso Lingis (Pittsburgh, PA: Duquesne University Press, 1969), 89; Emmanuel Levinas, *Otherwise Than Being* (Pittsburgh, PA: Duquesne, 2016), 59. I also really like Dietrich von Hildebrand's description of us as unique, "unrepeatable individuals" in Dietrich von Hildebrand, *The Nature of Love,* trans. John F. Crosby and John Henry Crosby (Notre Dame, IN: St. Augustine's Press, 2009), 203.

INDEX

action, xi, 4, 6, 8, 13, 56, 64–66, 138–39; phronetic action, 9–10, 14, 80–81, 113, 126, 130

aftercare, 33–34, 37–38

agency, 7, 15, 26, 112, 134, 146. *See also* fit; identity; intersectionality

Akrasia, 8–9, 15, 53, 80, 93, 112, 132, 135, 138, 145

anger, 53, 56, 66, 77; uses of, 150. *See also* creative maladjustment; passion; reasonable hostility

Arendt, Hannah, 138, 54

Aristotle, 9, 65–66, 80–81, 130, 133, 145–46, 150, 151, 153

audience, 23, 138, 141; audience integration, 27; target audience, 37

Bauman, Zygmunt, 7, 12, 145, 146

burnout, 3; myopia, 89. *See also* compassion fatigue

calling, 41, as in vocation, 80; conscience calling, 126, 134, 139

charity, 18, 26, 61, 67, 88

Cicero, 9. *See also* prudentia

collaboration, xii, 40, 51, 98, 127, 138

collective intelligence, 5; action, 14

community, 17–21, 26, 38, 40, 76, 79, 84, 96, 141; community activism, 47–48; kindness, 52–53, 59–61; organizers, 74; as support structure, 109

compassion fatigue, 37, 89. *See also* burnout

conscience, 126, 134, 152. *See also* calling; critical interruption

consumerism, 87–88, 91, 151

convention, 136, 146. *See also* norms

convergent thinking, 136–37, 154. *See also* divergent thinking

creative maladjustment, 66–67, 153. *See also* anger

Crenshaw, Kimberlé, 10–11, 146. *See also* intersectionality

critical interruption, 126–27, 132. *See also* calling

crowdsource, 2–4; the crowd, 4–5

curiosity, 7, 11, 29, 39, 101; as moral virtue or imperative, 39–40, 133, 148

Dewey, John, 9, 146

dilemma, 51. *See also* critical interruption; trickster

discernment, 13, 81, 113

divergent thinking, 136–138. *See also* convergent thinking; imagination

drift, 6–9, 13, 112, 144. *See also* liquid modernity; postmodernity

embodied action, 13, 132; performance, 23; knowledge, 94

epiphany, 21, 27, 86, 94

equity, 21, 88; contrasted with equality, 89; equity sharing, 92–93

Eudaemonia, 130, 139, 152. *See also* goodness

faith, 40–42, 109, 139. *See also* hope; trickster

fear, 2, 14, 35, 44–45, 52, 117; fearlessness, 64

fit, 6, 136; intersectional fit, 10–12. *See also* agency; intersectionality

folk music and tradition, xi, 143; folk performances, 22

global diaspora, 11, 146, 149; global corporations, 64; global war, 72

158 : Index

Rich, Adrienne, 4, 143, 146
right action, xi, 131, 138. *See also* phronesis; practical wisdom
Rilke, Rainer Maria, 28, 37, 100, 147, 151
risk, 8, 13, 48, 67, 80, 105, 125, 131; creative risk, 35; risk management, 93–94
Rumi: the poet, 118; the spice company, 123–28

security, xii, 11, 15, 67, 80, 111; climate security, 50
Self: the self, 11–13, 40, 132, 136, 146; self-awareness, 5, 10, 112; self-scrutiny, 26–28, 40, 131, 147; self-determination, 7; self-esteem, 23, 33, 76; self-importance, 28; self-respect, 19, 71. *See also* agency; fit; unselfing
showing up, 6–7, 13–14, 75, 108, 131
small: smallness, 29, 38, 40, 103, 113; small action, 138; small decisions, 125, 127, 151; small-scale, 4, 14, 21; small victories, 77
social media, 7, 145
Socrates, 8, 145
story: stories in the book, 3–4, 13–14, 131, 153, 141; the importance of storytelling, 3, 15, 72, 127, 133, 152
strangers, 11–14, 79, 131, 136–37, 147; strangerhood, 51–53
sustainability, 41, 43, 47, 54; sustain as maintain, enable, or support, 5, 20, 33–34, 39, 50, 90 110, 112, 141; sustained vigilance, 133–34; self-sustaining, 27

telos, 80–81, 94, 113, 130, 139
tonglen: meditation, 91–92
transcendence, 11
trickster, 52, 149
trust, 6, 7, 15, 19, 23, 26, 27, 40, 45, 47, 51, 77, 107, 113, 123, 131, 151; mistrust, 11, 46. *See also* vulnerability

uncertainty, 6, 8–9, 13, 112–13, 125, 137
unselfing, 13

vulnerability, 1, 7, 32, 112–13, 133, 151. *See also* liquid modernity; trust

war, xi, 2–3, 18, 32, 40, 50, 52, 71–73, 104, 106, 116–17, 120–21, 127, 129–30, 135, 143, 152; conflict's impact on environment, 43, 148
wayfinding, 143; feeling lost, xi, 6, 106. *See also* drift
Weil, Simone, 10, 146, 147, 150, 153
West, Cornel, 80–81, 143
Whitman, Walt, 10
wide-awakeness, 153. *See also* calling

zero-sum, 50, 72, 127, 152